THE STORY OF EMMELINE PANKHURST

Books by JOSEPHINE KAMM

YOUNG MOTHER

THE STORY OF FANNY BURNEY

THE STORY OF EMMELINE PANKHURST

Mrs. Pankhurst

The Story of EMMELINE PANKHURST

BY
JOSEPHINE KAMM

MEREDITH PRESS / New York

First U.S. edition

The photographs used in this book were made available through the kind cooperation of the Fawcett Library of London, England.

Photograph on page 86 copyright Elliott & Fry, Bassano, Vandyk. Used by permission.

Photograph on page 140 copyright W. Dennis Moss. Used by permission.

All other photographs reproduced by courtesy of Fawcett Library.

Library of Congress Catalog Card Number: 68-26328

MANUFACTURED IN THE UNITED STATES OF AMERICA FOR MEREDITH PRESS

VAN REES PRESS • NEW YORK

FOR

William and Belinda Bach

Contents

THE STORY OF
EMMELINE PANKHURST

CHAPTER 1

She Should Have Been a Boy

"WHAT a pity she wasn't born a lad!"

The child who overheard this remark, spoken by her father to her mother, stiffened with resentment as she lay in her bed pretending to be asleep. She kept her eyes closed while her father bent lovingly over her, shielding the flame of the candle he carried with one hand.

For days afterward the child pondered her father's remark. That he loved her dearly she knew, as much or more than any of his sons. Why, then, did he wish she had been a boy when she was perfectly content to be a girl? In the end she decided that he had really been paying her a compliment because all men—even the best—appeared to think themselves superior to women, and women did nothing to try and shake the men's belief in this ridiculous idea.

In a way her father's words rankled in the child's mind for the whole of her life, for she grew up to wage war against all those people who sought to deny women their rights and responsibilities. Her name was Emmeline Goulden, but she is remembered under her married name of Emmeline Pankhurst as the woman who fought by violent means for the right of women to vote on equal terms with men for their representatives in Parliament.

Emmeline Goulden was born in Manchester in July 1858. Her father, Robert Goulden, had begun his working life as an office boy, but he had worked his way up until now he owned a flourishing calico printing and bleach works. He was kind and broadminded—always full of ideas for helping the poor and the downtrodden. He was also very fond of amateur dramatics and became the leading Shakespearean actor in Manchester's dramatic society. His wife, the daughter of a farmer in Douglas in the Isle of Man, had been a beautiful girl, strong, energetic, and capable. The couple had ten children—five sons and five daughters. Emmeline was the eldest, Ada the youngest; and among the rest were Herbert, Robert and Walter, Mary, and Effie. The Gouldens lived in a large white house on the outskirts of Manchester, separated from Robert Goulden's factory by his own gardens and fields.

Mrs. Goulden spent much of her time in her dairy and kitchen, supervising the making of cream, butter, and cheese, and turning out prodigious quantities of jams, jellies, and pies. The children led a happy, sheltered life, with holidays at Douglas Bay on the Isle of Man. At Douglas they swam, rode ponies, went for long walks, and visited their grandmother, a great teller of stories.

As the eldest of the family Emmeline had to take a hand in looking after the little ones, and this meant that she grew up rather quickly. But in any event she was a natural leader, thoughtful and serious-minded and fond of listening to grown-up conversation. She learned easily, and at a very early age was reading the newspaper to her father while he ate his breakfast. "Here comes the walking dictionary," her younger brothers chanted when they saw her with a newspaper or book, for when she wrote she was never known to make a mistake in spelling.

There were plenty of books in the Goulden household, and before she was twelve Emmeline was reading everything she could lay hands on, from John Bunyan's *Pilgrim's Progress* and *Holy War* to Thomas Carlyle's *French Revolution.* Her mother's favorite was *Uncle Tom's Cabin,* Harriet Beecher Stowe's famous novel in defense of the downtrodden Negro slaves of America. She read the book again and again to the children, and her eldest daughter never forgot the excitement and sadness of the story. The Gouldens were delighted when slavery was abolished in America in 1865; and one of Emmeline's first memories was of being taken to a bazaar to help raise money for the recently freed slaves.

Carlyle's *French Revolution* was much stiffer reading than *Uncle Tom's Cabin.* Mrs. Goulden smiled indulgently when she discovered her daughter curled up in a chair, her nose buried in the book. Emmeline was such a pretty child, her mother thought, with her deep blue eyes, her olive-tinted skin, dark hair and fine, dark eyebrows. She hoped, though, the child was not going to grow up into one of those tiresomely clever women whom men found so annoying. But, when she asked her daughter why she found Carlyle so interesting, Emmeline replied that she had just been reading about the fall of the Bastille, the notorious French prison which, on July 14th, 1789, had been stormed by the people of Paris at the start of the French Revolution. Her own birthday was on July 14th, and that made her specially interested in the Revolution, she told her mother.

It was true that Emmeline was fascinated by all stories of people revolting against tyranny. Mrs. Goulden had seen her eyes sparkle when her father told her the story of *his* father. Emmeline's grandfather had been kidnapped as a boy by the pressgang, the body of sailors used to impress (or force) men to serve in the Navy when England was at war, and had returned home years later to find that his family and friends had all vanished. Later on, in 1819, he had nearly lost his life at St. Peter's Field in Manchester. He was one of the crowd which had gathered there to plead for parliamentary reforms. There was a clash with the military in which many innocent people were killed; the conflict went down in history as the Peterloo Massacre.

Mrs. Goulden's mother in the Isle of Man also had stories to tell, of the "Hungry Forties" of the nineteenth century when the price of corn was allowed to climb so high that poor people were plunged into the direst distress.

Tales like these filled Emmeline with a sense of the world's injustice, and she was only nine when she saw something which she considered desperately unjust herself. In Manchester a number of Irishmen started a riot in support of a rebellion against England by their fellow countrymen in Ireland. The leaders of the Manchester riot were arrested and taken to prison in a prison truck. On the way their friends stopped the truck and made an attempt to rescue them. A man fired a pistol at the locked door of the truck, killing a policeman who was sitting inside. Several men were promptly arrested for this crime and three were hanged for murder.

To Emmeline's parents this was a monstrous piece of injustice; the murder had not been planned and only one man had fired a shot. And to make matters even worse, the execution took place in public. When Emmeline passed the prison ground next day on her way home from the little school she attended she noticed the gap which had been torn in the wall so that people could watch the hanging. She stood gazing in horror through the gap into the empty prison ground; and as she stared she became sure that the execution had not simply been a mistake in judgment, as some people were saying, but a dreadful crime. "It was my awakening to one of the most terrible facts of life," she wrote many years later, "that justice and judgment lie often a world apart."

There was injustice of a lesser kind, so Emmeline thought, even in her own home. Although she was loved and protected and happy, her parents seemed quite unconcerned about her future education. There was a great deal of talk about sending the boys to the best available schools, but the question of schools for the girls was scarcely mentioned. At that time girls were given very little education, and professions and most of the jobs they do today were closed to them. Women were expected to marry young. Those who did not marry stayed at home, unless they belonged to the poorer classes, who worked long hours in mills or factories. No woman was thought capable of controlling money; when she married everything she possessed automatically became the property of her husband. There were, of course, enlightened people who thought this state of affairs unjust, but to the majority it seemed quite fair and proper.

It was not, therefore, very surprising that, although in many ways the Gouldens' ideas were in advance of their times, they thought less about the education of their daughters than that of their sons. The girls could read as much as they liked at home; and it would be a good thing, their parents considered, if they learned to speak a foreign language and could sing or play the piano or paint; but these subjects were enough for girls who were well looked after at home and would probably marry in their early twenties. Young as she was, Emmeline resented this attitude of her parents most bitterly. No one was more ready than they were to support good causes, but they saw no reason why their daughters should be equipped for life with all the benefits of a really sound education.

At home the girls learned far more than they did at school; and it was at home that Emmeline first heard discussed the question of the franchise, the right to vote. At that time no women, and not all men, had the vote, but the Gouldens believed strongly that women should have it. Under an act of Parliament, the Reform Bill of 1832, leaseholders—men who held houses or other property on a lease—paying a rent of not less than £10 a year in the towns and £50 in the counties were entitled to vote. Before 1832 the vote had been confined to property owners. A new reform bill passed in 1867 gave considerably more people the vote, extending it to all borough householders paying poor taxes for the support of the destitute, to lodgers paying £10 a year, and to tenants in counties paying £12. While the bill was being debated in Parliament a member of the House of Commons—the famous writer on politics and economics, John Stuart Mill—proposed that women leaseholders should be included. His proposal was defeated; but Mill and his friends believed that the bill contained a loophole. Instead of using the words "male person" to describe the new voters the bill used the word "man"; and "man" is often used with reference to men and women jointly. It therefore seemed possible that the framers of the bill had extended the franchise to women without meaning to do so.

In order to test this possibility a campaign was started to get women's names placed on the register; and in Manchester alone 3,924 women out of the 4,215 who might be entitled to vote sent in their claims. The women's claim was debated in the courts by a number of well-known lawyers and, although it was rejected, the discussions had drawn attention to the women's cause and brought it fresh sympathizers.

The Gouldens were among those who felt sure that although the women's claim had been rejected the passing of the Reform Bill was a step in the right direction. Emmeline, who at nine had very little idea what it meant, was caught up in the general excitement. Her parents were Liberals, and the Liberal Party stood for social progress. She had an idea that if the Liberals could win the next general election they would bring about many reforms.

When polling day arrived Emmeline decided that she ought to do something to help the Liberal candidate. She and Mary, the sister who came next to her in age, dressed themselves that morning in their new winter dresses. When they were ready they looked very much alike, for Mary resembled her elder sister in features and coloring.

"They're nice frocks," said Mary, fingering the warm material.

"They're green," said Emmeline with approval, "and our petticoats are red." She lifted the hem of her frock to show the red flannel petticoat beneath. "Green and red are the Liberal colors."

Mary looked pleased. "We are Liberals, aren't we?"

"Of course we are, and this gives us a chance to prove it."

"How can we do that?"

"Come along with me and I'll show you." A pink flush came into Emmeline's cheeks as she seized Mary by the hand. "Don't make a sound or someone will try and stop us."

Mary looked doubtful. "Where are we going, then?"

"Don't ask questions; you'll soon see."

All her life Mary was to follow Emmeline's lead; now she allowed herself to be hustled silently down the stairs and out of the house.

No one saw the children as they crept out of the garden gates into the road. "We're going to the polling booth," Emmeline announced, setting out in a determined way.

"What's that?" asked Mary, who had to trot to keep up with her sister.

"A polling booth is the place where the men go to vote."

"We can't go in there; we're not men."

"We're not going in," said Emmeline importantly. "We're going to demonstrate outside."

The nearest polling booth was about a mile away in a factory district. When the children arrived, Emmeline in front, Mary, rather red in the face, panting behind, they found a large crowd watching the voters go in and out. The crowd was noisy and inclined to be rough; it was made up mostly of out-of-work men, but there was a sprinkling of women with shawls drawn over ther heads.

Emmeline wormed her way through the crowd, dragging Mary behind her. "Look," she cried, pointing to a man standing outside the polling booth, "the Liberal colors."

The man, who was wearing a rosette of red and green, was clearly one of the Liberal candidate's officials because he kept popping in and out of the polling booth and issuing directions.

"Follow me," said Emmeline to Mary, "and do exactly what I do." She lifted the skirt of her dress so that the red flannel petticoat showed underneath, marched a few yards to the left, turned, and came strutting boldly back. She repeated the operation and this time Mary, her skirts clutched in her hand, marched solemnly behind her.

"Bless us, just take a look at the little lasses," cried a voice from the crowd.

There was a good deal of good-humored jostling and

craning of necks. "Wearing the Liberal colors and all," said another.

"Who are they? They shouldn't be allowed out," called one of the women.

"They're Bob Goulden's lasses, I'll be bound."

The children took no notice of the crowd but continued to march up and down.

Presently, however, Emmeline felt a heavy hand on her shoulder. She tried to break free but the hand held her too tightly; she looked up and saw the disapproving face of one of her mother's maids.

"Miss Emmeline, Miss Mary, what on earth do you think you're doing?"

"Demonstrating," said Emmeline firmly.

"Then you'll demonstrate home to bed. Come along at once, the two of you."

"How did you know we were here?" asked Emmeline as the maid hurried her charges homeward.

"We thought you were up in the schoolroom till a man with a red-and-green rosette came and knocked on the front door. Your mother's in a fine way, I can tell you."

It seemed very unfair to Emmeline. It's just because we're girls, she thought angrily. If we'd been boys they'd have let us do what we liked.

CHAPTER 2

Growing Up

SEVERAL years went by before Emmeline had her first real taste of politics. She arrived home from school one afternoon to find her mother just setting out for a meeting.

"What is the meeting about, Mother? May I come with you?"

"It's a meeting on women's suffrage," Mrs. Goulden explained. "Miss Lydia Becker, who founded our suffrage committee in Manchester, is going to speak. You're fourteen now, Emmeline, quite old enough to take an interest in the question of the women's vote. Yes, you may come along if you like."

The audience in the hall where the meeting was to take place was small and orderly. Miss Becker, a plain, severe-looking woman, wore steel-rimmed spectacles and a small black bonnet, with a black shawl over her plain black dress. She doesn't look like a public figure, thought Emmeline, who had pictured someone fiery and dramatic; yet she knew that it was Miss Becker who had been responsible for collecting the names of the women who had claimed the right to be put on the register after the passing of the Reform Bill. It did not take her long to find out that Lydia Becker was heart and soul behind the movement which demanded women's rights. She spoke earnestly and well of the struggle that lay ahead if women were to gain the privilege of voting. The day would come, she was sure, and meanwhile every right-thinking man and woman should work for it.

As she listened Emmeline felt a light break in on her. Women's suffrage was a cause worth fighting for. And she wrote of this meeting later on, "I left the meeting a confirmed suffragist."

There was not much she could do about it at the moment. Even if she had not been so young Emmeline was far too shy to dream of addressing meetings. Indeed, the bare idea of appearing in public made her quake with fear. At a performance at her school recently she had been billed to play a few bars on the piano alone; but when the time came she had been so scared that her hands would not move and one of the teachers had had to lean over her shoulders and play the notes for her. In an emergency, however, she was clearheaded enough. She was at school one afternoon when she noticed that a lighted lamp which hung from the ceiling had accidentally been detached from its socket. In another second the lamp would have fallen on the heads of a group of children at play; but in that second Emmeline had sprung forward and caught the falling lamp between her hands.

At about this time Mr. Goulden, who often went to France on business, decided—to Emmeline's delight and surprise—to send her to a finishing school in Paris. War between France and Germany had ended only the previous year, in 1871, in victory for Germany; and Paris still bore the scars of a four months' siege, which had reduced the population to starvation, and of the occupation by the conquering German army.

The school Mr. Goulden had chosen was the École Normale in the Avenue de Neuilly, one of the first schools opened for the higher education of girls. The head mistress, Mlle. Marchef-Girard, who was very much in advance of her day, believed that girls should have as good an education as boys, and she included bookkeeping, chemistry, and other sciences in her syllabus as well as embroidery and more "ladylike" subjects.

It was holiday time when Mr. Goulden deposited Emmeline on the doorstep of the house in the Avenue de Neuilly. All the girls were away except one—a tall, fair, and very beautiful girl a few years older than Emmeline whose name was Noémie Rochefort. Noémie's mother was dead; her father, who called himself Henri Rochefort, was a Communist who never used his name and title—the Marquis de Rochefort-Luçay. Henri Rochefort had been a leader of the Paris Commune, which had tried to rule after the German troops had been withdrawn. A rising by the Commune against the Government had resulted in civil war; the Commune had been defeated, and Henri Rochefort had been sentenced to transportation for life to the island of New Caledonia, a French colony in the South Pacific.

The two girls became firm friends in the few weeks which passed before the other pupils returned; and Emmeline was fascinated by Noémie's stories of the Commune and her father's part in the ill-fated rising. Some time later—after two years' imprisonment—he managed to escape from New Caledonia in an open boat and had the great good fortune to be picked up by an American liner and carried to freedom.

In the meantime Noémie and Emmeline were exploring Paris. The elder girl hated work; the younger was considered by the school doctor to be too delicate to be troubled with many lessons. So, while the English girl learned to chatter fluently in French, the scientific subjects taught in the school passed her by. If she had any regrets she did not say so, for she adored Paris and never tired of talking to Noémie.

Emmeline was seventeen when she came home from Paris. She looked very grown-up in her long dresses, and she moved with the grace and elegance of a Frenchwoman. Mrs. Goulden thought her most unusual looking, with her slim, erect figure, her deep blue eyes, very dark hair and eyebrows, and the color which tinged her olive-toned cheeks when she was moved or excited.

But Emmeline was something of a problem. Her brothers' friends admired her; but they were too young to be taken seriously and, privately, she found them rather dull. She wanted to work, to do something glorious for the women's cause; yet there she was, cooped up at home with nothing special to do.

"I envy you, Mary," she told her favorite sister, who was to go in her turn to the École Normale. "You have

Paris ahead of you, and I'd give almost anything to go back."

"How I wish you could," said Mary, who was as fond of her elder sister as she had been as a child. "Shall I ask Father if you can?"

Emmeline would never allow other people to do her work for her. "I'll ask him myself," she replied, laughing. "After all, he can't eat me."

Rather to Emmeline's surprise Mr. Goulden needed no persuasion. If his eldest daughter thought another year at school would make her happy, she should have it. She was still very young, he thought; there was plenty of time to think of the future.

And so when Mary went to Paris the following year Emmeline went with her. It was almost like going home, and in Paris she found a second home, for her friend Noémie Rochefort was now married and had a home and a baby daughter of her own. Noémie's husband, a young Swiss, was an artist who was struggling to make his way in the world, and Noémie, who did not mind being poor, managed to keep open house for her husband's artist friends.

"Life would be altogether perfect," Noémie told Emmeline, "if you could marry a Frenchman and come and live near us."

Emmeline gazed at her friend, who was as fair and lovely as ever but growing a little plump. Noémie had just finished putting the baby to bed. Still in her apron, she had lifted the lid from the stockpot simmering on the stove, which filled the large room that served as living room, studio, and kitchen with a savory smell. "Would you like to marry a Frenchman?" asked Noémie as she replaced the lid.

"Of course I should like to live near you," said Emmeline, "but how shall I set about it? First I should have to find a husband, and that might not be easy."

"The easiest thing in the world. You know the friend who was here the other evening"—and Noémie mentioned the name of a friend of her husband's whom Emmeline had met several times—"Well, he's charming and ambitious and certain to make his name as a writer. He admires you immensely, and I'm quite sure a marriage could be arranged if you wanted it; and think what a brilliant hostess you would make to all his important literary friends!"

The idea of herself as a brilliant hostess appealed to Emmeline, and it was true that she had liked the young writer very much. All the same, she was a little doubtful. "Arranged, you say, Noémie? Doesn't an arranged marriage sound a little . . . well, matter-of-fact and unromantic? You married for love, didn't you?"

"We did, and just look at us, as poor as church mice. But you know as well as I do that in France a great many marriages are arranged, and very happy marriages they are, too. I'm almost certain that if we speak to the young man he'll be overjoyed, because he's already given us several hints. Then all we shall have to do is to ask your father how big a dowry he can afford for you."

Emmeline drew her fine black eyebrows together in a frown. She had an uneasy feeling that her father would not approve of the idea of settling money on her. "Hmmmm," she said doubtfully, "we shall have to see."

The young man, when approached by Noémie's husband, said he would be charmed to marry Emmeline. She would make an ideal wife for a writer, and if the small matter of the dowry could be settled satisfactorily, he was convinced they would be exceedingly happy.

But when Emmeline wrote explaining all this to her father she received an indignant reply. Mr. Goulden generally so indulgent, refused point-blank to give his daughter to any man who wanted her for her money. If the young man loved her he would marry her without a dowry; if he refused, then it was a sign that he did not love her.

It was in vain for Emmeline to argue that all married women should have money of their own; her father was adamant. As for the young man, when he learned that the delightful English girl could not expect a dowry, he swiftly withdrew his offer of marriage.

"You are to come home at once," wrote Mr. Goulden, when he received this piece of information, which was precisely what he had expected. And Emmeline, furious with the young man and still more furious with her father, had no choice but to say good-bye to Noémie and her husband and return to Manchester.

Mary Goulden was also home again by this time, and some weeks after Emmeline's arrival the sisters held an indignation meeting in the bedroom which they shared at the top of the house. Mary was gifted and artistic. She wanted to go on the stage, but her plea to be an actress had been decisively turned down by her father on the grounds that no well-brought-up girl ever went on the stage. Instead, she had been concentrating on painting, and earlier that evening had run excitedly to her parents with the news that one of the local shops was prepared to take some of her pictures and put them on sale.

Instead of being pleased, as Mary had hoped, Mr. Goulden had been extremely annoyed. What on earth would his business friends say, he demanded, if they knew that Robert Goulden's daughter was actually trying to sell her paintings? Mary thought they would be interested, perhaps a trifle jealous that their own daughters were not so enterprising. Mr. Goulden said, "Nothing of the sort." His friends would imagine that he was short of money, and no rumor could be more damaging to a businessman. Mary must go back at once and tell the shopkeeper that her work was not for sale.

And so the two sisters had gone upstairs to pour out their unhappiness and disappointment to one another.

"It's the injustice of it," cried Mary, marching up and down the comfortably furnished room as though it were a prison cell. "If Father was a poor man he would be glad enough for me to earn some money. The boys are being trained for the business, but just because he can afford to keep us girls at home he refuses to let me have any sort of career."

"Father could perfectly well have afforded to give me a dowry," countered Emmeline, who was still harping on her own grievance. "If only he had I should have been married by now and you could have come to us in Paris and gone on with your painting."

Mary paused in her marching. "It's no use crying over spilled milk, I suppose. We shall just have to resign ourselves to doing nothing."

"You're a softer person than I am, Mary. I can't and won't resign myself to injustice. Do you know what Mother told me when I asked her how we were expected to occupy our time?" she demanded, a shrill note of sarcasm in her rather deep voice. "She said we could try and make home attractive to our brothers. Did you ever hear such ridiculous nonsense?"

"And how does she expect us to do that?" asked Mary, who could not refrain from laughing.

"Apparently by bringing them their slippers when they come back in the evening."

There was such a look of disgust on Emmeline's face that Mary stopped laughing. "You would think" she said, "that Mother could have thought of something a little more original."

"Oh, she did. She suggested that we might take turns dusting the drawing room and arranging the flowers. That Mother of all people should imagine that we could be contented with such dull and aimless duties. She talks so much about women's rights, yet her own daughters have no rights at all. All we are to be allowed to do is to fetch and carry our brothers' slippers until such time as suitable husbands present themselves, after which we shall be doomed to spend the rest of our days fetching and carrying slippers for our husbands."

"At least we can take an interest in good causes," said Mary, "and go to meetings."

"I'm sick and tired of meetings. I want to do something, and be somebody."

It was in this frame of mind that a few evenings later Emmeline reluctantly agreed to accompany her parents to a meeting. The previous year, 1877, Russia had declared war on Turkey, and there was some talk of Britain's intervening on the side of Turkey. The Gouldens were opposed to war. So, too, was the chief speaker at the meeting, Dr. Richard Marsden Pankhurst, who was also the leader of the Manchester peace party.

Dr. Pankhurst, a Doctor of Laws of London University, was the son of a Manchester auctioneer. He had been educated at Manchester University—then called Owens College after its founder, John Owens—and afterward at London; and he had qualified both as a solicitor and a barrister. Scholarly and idealistic, Dr. Pankhurst had taken up the cause of women's suffrage as long ago as 1867; for it was under his leadership that after the passage of the Reform Bill the campaign was waged to get women's names on the register. In addition, he had been one of the eminent lawyers who had argued the case in the courts.

At that time Dr. Pankhurst had been just past thirty, and Emmeline Goulden had been nine; now he was forty-two and she was twenty.

Emmeline was standing with her parents on the steps of the hall when a cab drove up. She saw a hand, a beautiful hand, she recalled afterwards, emerge from the window to open the cab door. There was a burst of cheering from the assembled crowd as Dr. Pankhurst alighted and strode up the steps. At the top he was confronted by the slight, erect figure of Emmeline. She blushed with confusion, which made her look more vivid and even prettier than usual; and although he passed on quickly into the hall he did not forget her.

The Gouldens admired Richard Pankhurst immensely for his eloquence and for his championship of the causes which they held dear. As for Emmeline, she fell immediately and genuinely in love with this man, with his gentle, bearded face and lively manner, who was old enough to be her father. At first she felt hopelessly ignorant and quite unable to talk to someone who was learned and had years of public service to his credit. But she soon found that he was as much in love with her as she was with him.

Richard Pankhurst had made up his mind years ago to remain unmarried for the sake of his work, but his meetings with Emmeline Goulden made him think differently. In her he knew he had found someone who would be glad to work with him, who would make his causes hers.

"Dear Miss Goulden," he wrote soon after they met. "There is now in action an important movement for the higher education of women. As one of the party of progress, you must be interested in this." And he went on to enlist her help in framing a scheme which would make such education efficient and real.

This letter was written on September 8. By September 23 they were engaged to be married and Emmeline was his "Dearest Treasure" when he wrote to thank her for her photograph. "The fire and soul of the original can never consent to enter a copy," he continued. "Still, when the original is absent, the copy consoles and animates."

Their engagement was to be a short one. The wedding day was fixed, and Mary and three younger sisters were to be Emmeline's bridesmaids. The girls were happily planning their dresses when Dr. Pankhurst's mother was taken seriously ill and died after a brief illness.

There was no question of postponing the wedding, but it took place very quietly. There were no bridesmaids, and instead of wearing white satin, with a veil and orange blossom in her dark hair, Emmeline Goulden was married in a plain brown velvet dress.

CHAPTER 3

Marriage and Partnership

DESPITE the difference in their ages the Pankhursts were exceedingly happy, but in the early days of their marriage Emmeline was worried because Richard seemed so learned and she was so ignorant.

"Your friends will think you've married a fool," she said after an evening of legal talk which she had been quite unable to understand. "You must make me a study program of books and pamphlets to read, and then at least I shall know what it's all about."

An ordinary husband would have told his wife not to worry her pretty little head about matters which did not concern her; but Richard Pankhurst was an upholder of the rights of women and, besides, he had the greatest respect for his young wife's intelligence. He did as she asked and made out an elaborate course for her. For a few weeks Emmeline studied diligently, then impatiently threw it aside. She wanted action, not dry-as-dust books. Life was an exciting adventure and if sometimes domestic work was a little humdrum she could turn for excitement to novels.

Watching her as she picked up one novel after another,

reading here and there as the fancy took her, Richard smiled and raised his eyebrows. "Have you the slightest idea, my dearest, what any of these novels is about?"

"Of course I know what they're about," answered Emmeline, eyes sparkling, cheeks flushed. And she proceeded to tell him the plot of novel after novel until he begged her to stop.

"You certainly know how to tear the heart out of a book," he said admiringly. "You may find it a very useful asset one of these days."

"Can I make it useful to your work, Richard?"

"I am sure you can."

In later years friends were to admire the speed and accuracy with which Emmeline could wade through a pile of newspapers, picking out all the items of importance and interest without a moment's hesitation.

In the meantime, before work came the children. During the first five years of her married life Emmeline had four children—two girls, Christabel and Sylvia, then a son, Henry Francis, who was known as Frank, and another daughter, Adela. Before the birth of the last baby the family lived for a time with Emmeline's parents. The little girls, Christabel and Sylvia, were thoroughly spoiled by their five uncles and four aunts, the youngest of whom—Ada—was only twelve years old at the time. At Christmas the uncles and aunts produced a pantomime. Sylvia was Cinderella, in a pink tulle balldress which she found in the attic; Christabel was the prince; and two of the uncles played the part of an elephant, so that, instead of going to the ball in a glass coach, Cinderella traveled on an elephant's back.

The birth of her youngest daughter, Adela, left Emmeline weak and worn, with headaches and poor digestion from which she suffered for the rest of her life. The children had a devoted nurse called Susan Jones, a capable, motherly Welshwoman. Susan not only looked after the children but her mistress and the housekeeping as well, for Emmeline, who never had any money sense, soon realized that Susan could make the housekeeping money go much farther than she could.

The Pankhursts were always hard up, although they would not have been if Dr. Pankhurst had concentrated on his career as a lawyer. But his head was so full of schemes to help the working people of the country achieve a better standard of living and to gain for women the rights and privileges enjoyed by men, that he gave his time freely to any good cause. Because some of his ideas—especially his ideas on women's suffrage—were considered outrageous or ridiculous, Dr. Pankhurst was looked on as something of a crank. People accused him of being a Socialist with dangerously advanced ideas, and in those days it was unwise for a man to have advanced ideas if he wanted to be a success at the Bar.

Emmeline was perfectly content for Richard to follow his own ideals, whatever people might say or think. She wanted to see him achieve great things, and she longed to help him. Not long after their marriage, and while the children were still tiny, she began to do some suffrage work on her own. The Manchester branch of the Women's

Suffrage Society elected her to their committee. She was also appointed to a committee which was trying to get a bill introduced into Parliament to ensure that married women could keep their own property and money instead of being obliged to hand it over automatically to their husbands.

Richard, thought Emmeline, must go into Parliament. Only in the House of Commons could he really make his mark and do the work he loved best. Perhaps she thought of herself as a political hostess, as once she had pictured herself as hostess in Paris to a famous writer, for she certainly wanted to make her own mark in the world. In any event she was full of enthusiasm when her husband decided to fight a by-election in Manchester. A Liberal Government was in office at the time under the great Prime Minister William Ewart Gladstone, and Richard Pankhurst, whose views differed in some ways from those of the Government, stood as an Independent Liberal. Emmeline worked hard in her husband's election campaign, and her father acted as his agent; and she was bitterly disappointed when he was decisively beaten at the polls.

Two years later he tried again, this time as the official Liberal candidate for the riverside London district of Rotherhithe. He was beaten once more. Although he took his defeat well Emmeline was despondent; she had been so certain that Parliament would provide an outlet for his gifts and increase his influence on public affairs. She was restless, too, and much as she loved her children, she was not the kind of woman to make a full life for herself within the walls of her home. The suffrage work interested her intensely, but she had grown tired of Manchester. This was partly because she was no longer on good terms with her father, who feared that Dr. Pankhurst was veering away from the Liberal Party into a dangerous form of Socialism and carrying Emmeline with him. Mr. Goulden was a staunch Liberal, and it was certainly true that his son-in-law's views were losing him influential clients.

So the Pankhursts left Manchester for London. With them went the faithful Susan Jones and Emmeline's sister, Mary. Richard Pankhurst had offices in London, but he knew that his work would often take him to Manchester. As for Emmeline, she had a plan to help with the family budget. She and Mary would open a shop and sell all sorts of beautiful things—lampshades, silks, and pottery. Mary, who was artistic, would decorate some of the goods with her flower paintings, and because the things they sold would be lovely and unusual Emmeline was sure their venture would be a success.

"It will be something more than just a shop," she told her husband. "If we make it pay it will show that women can be as good in business as men, and once people realize that women are equal to men in business and the professions, they won't be able to deny us the vote much longer."

Naturally Richard agreed. "If women are going to get the vote," he said, "they must prove themselves fitted to use it. And if you and Mary succeed with your shop it will be a step in the right direction."

It did not take Emmeline long to find her shop. It was on Hampstead Road, not far from Tottenham Court Road, and there were rooms above in which the family could live. She proceeded to stock it will all kinds of fancy goods, painted wooden milking stools and photograph frames as well as silks, lampshades, and pottery.

The sisters called their shop Emerson & Company. Emmeline was full of enthusiasm and energy, but customers were few. Londoners flocked to Shoolbred's, a large shop on nearby Tottenham Court Road, but Hampstead Road was in a poor district, a center for shops selling low-priced food, and quite unsuitable for a fancy-goods shop. Try as they might, Emmeline and Mary made no headway, and Emmeline, impatient when things went wrong, began to talk of giving up. But her husband reassured her; he was more patient and deliberate than she was, and he still felt that the shop might be the start of something really big.

Because business was so slow Emmeline sometimes used to leave Mary in charge and go with her husband to Manchester, where so much of his legal work remained. Thus, when he told her that he was acting in an important inquiry which would keep him out of London for several weeks, she decided that he should not go alone.

They had been in Manchester only a few days when a telegram arrived. Frank, their only son, was very ill.

"I must go home at once," said Emmeline.

"Of course, my dear. If only I could go with you, but I can't possibly leave until the inquiry is over."

Dr. Pankhurst hated to have to stay. He loved all his children, but bright, intelligent four-year-old Frank was his favorite. "You will have Mary and Susan to help you," he told his wife as they said good-bye at the railway station, "but I wish I could be there to share the responsibility."

When Emmeline reached home, late on a cold afternoon, she found the two elder girls, Christabel aged eight, and Sylvia, six, huddled together on the stairs.

"Frank's got a sore throat," said Christabel, a round-faced, rosy-cheeked child. "Susan says it's croup."

Emmeline hugged the little girls, who followed her upstairs.

"Aunt Mary says we mustn't see Frank in case his sore throat's catching," said Christabel.

"She's quite right. Go and play in the nursery and I'll come to you as soon as I can."

The children brightened a little, but Sylvia clutched at her mother's long skirts as though she dreaded to see her go.

The blinds had been drawn in Frank's room, which was lighted only by nightlights, one by the bed, another on the chest of drawers. As Emmeline came into the room Susan rose from her chair at the bedside, her face drawn and worried.

"Thank God you've come, Ma'am," she whispered. "The poor little lad's not at all well this evening."

The two women bent over the bed. Frank's eyes were closed; he looked very pale and he breathed with difficulty.

When Emmeline took his hand Frank opened his eyes. "My throat hurts so," he said.

"You'll be better soon, my darling," his mother promised. "Shut your eyes and try to sleep."

She beckoned Susan out of the room. "What does the doctor say? Has he been this evening?"

"He'll be here any minute. But he's not *our* doctor, you know. Our own man's away till the day after tomorrow, and strange doctors don't understand."

When the doctor arrived he told Emmeline that Frank was not seriously ill. "Croup can be very distressing, but it's nothing to worry about. The child will be much better in the morning, you'll find."

Emmeline sat up with Frank all night. He was terribly restless, and in the morning he was no better.

The doctor came and went, still full of confidence. In the evening he returned with his partner, but neither man could see, what Emmeline felt in her bones, that Frank was desperately ill.

Susan insisted on sitting up with Frank that night because Emmeline was so tired she could scarcely keep her eyes open. "Our own man will be here in the morning, Ma'am," she said comfortingly. "He'll take care of the lad, never fear."

The mere sight of the tall, fatherly doctor they had come to know well brought a feeling of security to Christabel and Sylvia, who were at their usual vantage point on the stairs. They had not been told that Frank was really ill, but they were old enough to sense that something was very wrong.

"You'll make Frank better, won't you?" said Christabel, and her voice was so trustful that the doctor had no need to reply.

He disappeared into the sickroom with Emmeline and

Susan, and was gone a long time. When he emerged his face was very grave and sad. "You girls will be a great help to your mother now," was all he said.

But eight-year-old Christabel, feeling suddenly twice her age, knew that her brother was dead.

Emmeline was brokenhearted. She was also extremely angry because the other doctors had diagnosed her son's illness as croup when he had had diphtheria, which was exceedingly dangerous. "How could he have caught the infection," she asked, "when the children are so well looked after?"

The doctor countered with another question. "Did you think to have the drains of the house examined before you took it?" he said. "The neighborhood is not a particularly healthy one."

Emmeline shook her head. She had been so pleased with the comfortable rooms above the shop that she had not thought of the drainage, which in the 1880's was often a source of infection. "The other children should be moved away, then?"

"It would certainly be advisable until we know if the drains are safe."

The three little girls were immediately packed off with Susan to furnished rooms in Richmond.

Diphtheria, as we now know, is caused by a particular germ and the injections which all children can have today make it impossible for them to get the disease. While nobody could be sure that Frank's illness had been caused by the drains, they were found to be badly defective, and

Emmeline decided that the children must stay away until she could find another house.

She found what she wanted not far away on Russell Square, but she was too wretchedly unhappy at first to take much interest in the new house. She blamed herself most bitterly for Frank's death. If she had not insisted on living in such a miserable district, she thought, he would never have caught diphtheria. Then her mind turned from her own trouble to anger against the hardship and poverty which forced people to live in such unhealthy surroundings, and she knew that she must fight against these conditions so that the world could be made a better and a safer place for the children of the future.

CHAPTER 4

Early Work

EMMELINE soon found plenty of work to do and London seemed full of fellow workers. The new house in Russell Square had a double drawing room large enough for conferences, and before long men and women concerned with the question of women's rights and other social and political problems were meeting there regularly.

The Pankhursts had broken with the Liberal Party when Prime Minister Gladstone refused to put women's suffrage into the Reform Bill of 1884, and they had joined the newly founded Fabian Society, a group of British Socialists.

In spite of her first failure Emmeline opened another shop, on Berners Street, off Oxford Street. She stocked it with goods which were fashionable at the time—Persian pottery plates, Oriental brasses and embroidery, and white painted furniture with fretwork decoration. For a short while the shop did well enough, but when the novelty wore off business began to slow down and Dr. Pankhurst had to pay to keep it going. The Pankhursts would have been better off without the shop, just as they would if Dr. Pankhurst had not given so much time and money to public causes; and the shop might have prospered if Emmeline had not given so much of her attention to other work. But this was the way they had chosen to live, and for them it was the only way.

At the Russell Square house Emmeline's fifth child—a second son—was born, and to father and mother it was almost as though Frank had been born again. They called the baby by their dead son's names, Henry Francis, but he was known as Harry, not Frank.

Harry's birth nearly cost Emmeline her life. She was taken ill a few days afterward, so ill that she appeared to be dying. For the second time in an emergency the Pankhursts' doctor was away. While Mary kept the older children amused, Susan rushed out into the street in search of another doctor, the strings of her starched white cap flying like a flag of distress. She tried the houses of several doctors, only to be told that the doctor was out on his rounds or could not take on somebody else's patient. Finally she forced her way into a house and stormed into the room where a doctor was eating his breakfast, crying despairingly, "My mistress is dying."

No doctor could ignore such an appeal; thanks to Susan's presence of mind, Emmeline was given the treatment which probably saved her life. She recovered quickly, but although she had plenty of energy, she was very easily exhausted and often had to drive herself to get through the day's work.

Politics—women's suffrage particularly—was the chief topic of conversation in the house on Russell Square. When a Women's Franchise League was started Emmeline was one of its first members; to her the vote was vital, something which women must have. To Christabel and Sylvia, now eleven and nine, a political meeting was far more exciting than films or television to a later generation. Ever since they were tiny they had been playing imaginary election games, and now they were allowed to attend some of the meetings held in their own home. Like many other children they started a paper, which they wrote entirely themselves. It was called *The Home News,* but instead of describing schoolroom and nursery happenings, it dealt with political meetings and receptions. According to the paper, Mrs. Pankhurst always "looked elegant in a trained evening gown." And on one occasion, "the Misses Pankhurst wore white crêpe dresses with worked yokes . . . and the refreshments were delicious, the strawberries and cream being especially so."

Christabel was already showing a businesslike interest in women's suffrage. "Mrs. Pankhurst held an At Home in her beautiful house on May 28," she wrote. "There was a great number of people there. Dr. Pankhurst, as chairman, said in his speech that if the suffrage was not given to women, the result would be terrible. If a body was half bound, how was it to be expected that it would grow and develop properly? This body was the human race and the fettered half, women."

Emmeline took great pains to make her receptions entertaining as well as serious, for she wanted to attract to them people who might find a whole evening of political talk rather heavy going. There was music and refreshments as well as speeches, and the gatherings were presided over by a hostess who wore a beautiful evening dress with a long train hanging from the shoulders.

At first it was agony to Emmeline to speak in public. Even to get up at a meeting and say, "I second the resolution," made her heart thump and her mouth feel dry. But she realized that if she was going to be of any real use in the political world she must learn to speak easily and well. I am going to be of use, she told herself, and I am going to work until women get the vote. She had several assets which at first she did not fully understand. The first was her appearance, and she soon grew accustomed to admiring looks. She was a beautiful woman, with her finely cut features, dark hair and deep blue eyes, and her slender, erect figure. Then, too, she had a lovely, expressive voice, and she learned to control it like a musical instrument. It was exciting and exhilarating to discover that she could sway an audience with her voice. It was even more exhilarating to find that people seemed eager to accept her leadership. There was something in her personality which drew them to her and made them willing to follow and serve her. This was particularly true of women, for there were few men then—as now—prepared to take orders from a woman.

As Christabel and Sylvia grew older their parents began to talk to them more seriously about their work. Both girls were convinced that women ought to have the vote, and Christabel, at any rate, thought that victory would come sooner if the battle was left to the young.

"How long you women have been trying for the vote,"

she told her mother impatiently one day. "For my part, I mean to get it."

At first Emmeline was inclined to tell her daughter that she had no idea what she was talking about. Then she paused to think. Was there, perhaps, a difference between trying for the vote and actually gaining it? Were some of the older workers getting tired and stale, and would they not have more chance of success if they joined hands with the young? Instead of snubbing Christabel, who looked extremely determined with her round, rosy face and her bright blue eyes, she smiled at her warmly.

"I believe you're right, Christabel," she said. "We older women need you because you're young and brave, and you need us because we have experience behind us. Together we shall fight and win."

The days of drawing-room meetings and receptions in London were coming to an end. The lease of the house on Russell Square was running out, and the owner had decided to pull the house down and build a hotel on the site. Dr. Pankhurst's health was not as good as it had been and he was finding it more and more trying to travel constantly between London and Manchester; as they grew older husband and wife hated their frequent separations even more than they had in the past. If Emmeline's shop had been a success they might have stayed on in London, but it had long since become a burden and there was really no reason why it should not be closed.

Once more the Pankhursts turned north. They spent a bleak winter at the Lancashire seaside town of Southport, with Dr. Pankhurst traveling to and from Manchester. Then they took rooms in a farmhouse in the Cheshire hills, where for the summer months Emmeline flung herself eagerly into country life. She went haymaking and harvesting, drove her children about in a pony-drawn trap, and went blackberrying with a zeal which bored and exhausted her daughters.

Dr. Pankhurst must often have wondered how long this kind of existence would hold his politically minded wife, and he could not have been surprised when she suddenly started spending most of her time at meetings and committees in Manchester. Before long Emmeline made up her mind that the family should move from the country to the town. She found a house which she liked in the Victoria Park district of Manchester. After one summer on the farm, the Pankhursts left the country for good.

The girls were now sent to Manchester High School. There had been no question of sending them to boarding school, for they would have hated to leave their parents and all the political meetings and activities which made life so exciting. Christabel and Sylvia loved their new home. Every evening they brought their homework to the gold-and-brown-papered library with its book-lined walls. They worked at a large table in the middle of the room. On one side of the fireplace sat their mother, with her books, her writing and sewing; on the other their father, with the legal books he was studying for his cases. And the girls often noticed that, however busy he might be, their father would stretch out a hand toward them every now and then as if to show that he liked having his family about him. If either of them needed help with her homework he would immediately leave his own work to hunt for references in the books on the shelves.

There was a glow of contentment about those winter evenings in Manchester which the girls never forgot. But the comfort of their own home did not blind the Pankhursts to the miseries outside. That winter—1894—was a bitter one, and in Manchester there was a great deal of unemployment. In those days there was no unemployment insurance and no unemployment relief except admission to the workhouse where paupers were housed. Because there were so many hungry people in the city that winter the Pankhursts set up a relief committee. Emmeline went daily to the market to beg the shopkeepers for vegetables, meat, and bones, which were then made into soup in vast caldrons and served to the unemployed. She also formed a women's subcommittee to help care for the mothers and children.

There was plenty of other work as well. There were outdoor meetings of the Suffrage Society to be organized so that working people could be encouraged to take an interest in their rights and privileges. And, when audiences had grown large enough, the Free Trade Hall was hired and filled to overflowing with earnest, enthusiastic listeners.

Like a number of other prominent women, Emmeline was also taking part in local affairs. Liberal Party leaders had suggested that if women wanted to prove that they were fit to vote they might do so by serving without pay on local boards of guardians, school boards and other bodies.

Emmeline Pankhurst had been elected a member of the Board of Poor Law Guardians for the large district of Chorlton-upon-Medlock. Under the Poor Laws of the day, money collected by taxes was used for the relief of the poor. The Guardians had the job of dispensing the money and also of building and controlling the workhouses, which housed many out-of-work families as well as the old and the ill.

People dreaded being sent to the workhouse because it was a sign that they were absolutely destitute. They hated it, too, because families were broken up, husbands and wives parted. Conditions were often extremely bad, and the inmates poorly clothed and fed.

The workhouse in the Chorlton district was a large one; it had a hospital with nine hundred beds, a school for several hundred children, a farm, and a large number of workshops.

When Emmeline became a Poor Law Guardian it did not take her long to make up her mind that the Board was trying to save by providing the workhouse inmates with poor-quality food, and also that, despite their efforts at economy, a great deal of food was being wasted. As soon as she felt sure of her ground she raised the question at a meeting of the Board.

"It seems to me," she said rather diffidently, "that the people in the workhouse have far too much bread in their diet."

"Bread is very filling," said one of the other Guardians.

"It's filling, I agree, but is it nourishing? And, since so much of it is left, it is obvious that people don't want it."

"The left-over bread is given to the pigs, Mrs. Pankhurst. As you know, we keep pigs in order to finish it."

"But pigs," said Emmeline, "thrive no more than human beings on a diet of stale bread. I'm told that our workhouse pigs fetch a far lower price in the market than pigs that are properly fed."

Nobody could deny this, and Emmeline was asked what she would suggest to solve the problem. Her idea was that, instead of handing out a loaf of uncut bread to each inmate, the loaves should be cut into slices, spread with margarine, and the inmates told they could eat as many slices as they wished. If there was any bread left over—and she thought it was unlikely that many people would eat a whole loaf—it could be made into puddings with milk and currants, and the money saved on bread could be spent on a little extra meat.

Several of the Guardians were doubtful about Emmeline's idea. "The inmates are very jealous of their rights," said one, "and they might think we were trying to cut their bread ration."

In the end, however, they decided to let the workhouse people decide. They all chose Emmeline's idea, which, when put into practice, did something to improve the quality of their food.

Emmeline found her colleagues on the Board as keen as she was to improve conditions. During the next few years she was in the forefront of a number of workhouse reforms. Proper chairs were provided for the old people instead of backless benches; warm dresses were given to the girls in the school, who had previously worn thin cotton frocks summer and winter; a system of cottage homes were started for the children out in the country; and a more modern school was built, staffed with trained teachers, and with a gymnasium and a swimming pool.

These reforms were important but they did not change the system.

"What's the use of a system which gives the children of the rich so much and the poor almost nothing?" she demanded passionately. "I want working people to have the good things of life." Emmeline discussed this with some of the leaders of the recently formed Independent Labor Party, who often came to the house in Victoria Park. She and her husband were strongly drawn toward labor and in due course they both joined the Party.

Dr. Pankhurst had hesitated for some time; even when he was only suspected of having Socialist leanings, his practice at the Bar had suffered. But he was a man of great moral courage and, once having decided to become a member of the I.L.P., he agreed to stand as Labor candidate for West Gorton, a working-class district of Manchester.

There were still very few Labor Members in the House of Commons, and no one was very surprised when Dr. Pankhurst was defeated at the polls. Had he been elected, his long years of experience in legal and public work would have been of considerable help to his party. Naturally, he was disappointed, but he had never yet let disappointment sour him, so he returned quietly to his work.

Quite soon after the election Emmeline went for a

holiday abroad. It had always been understood between her and her school friend, Noémie Rochefort, now Madame Rochefort-Dufaux, that if they had daughters the girls should pay exchange visits. As she was the eldest daughter, Christabel was going to spend a year with Noémie in Geneva; and Emmeline was to go with her and spend a few weeks with her old friend.

Noémie and Emmeline had plenty to talk about, for they had met very seldom since their school days. Noémie, once so fair and lovely, was still good-looking, but she had grown stout and matronly, whereas Emmeline was as slim and upright as she had been as a girl and looked far too young to have a grown-up daughter. Noémie was extremely happy running her household and organizing the lives of her husband and children; she had little time to spare for anything that went on outside her own family affairs. She had certainly changed. But the man whom Emmeline had once wanted to marry was still more changed. The charming, ambitious young writer who had refused to marry Emmeline without a dowry was now living in Geneva, and Noémie reintroduced him to her friend. He had grown enormously fat and middle-aged, and Emmeline found him "a dreadful creature." The mere idea that she might be married to him and not to Richard made her feel quite faint.

Emmeline's eyes brightened as she remembered the letter she had received from Richard only that morning. "When you return we will have a new honeymoon. Be happy. Love and love, Your husband, R. M. Pankhurst."

Two or three days later Emmeline and Noémie were in

the garden with Christabel and Noémie's children when a telegram was handed to Emmeline. She opened it and turned very pale.

"It's from Sylvia," she said. "It says, 'Father ill. Come at once.' "

"I do hope it's not serious," said Noémie anxiously.

"It may be nothing very much, but Sylvia is only fifteen and can't take the responsibility. Noémie, my dear, I must go home immediately."

Christabel offered to go with her, but Emmeline shook her head.

"You mustn't interrupt your year in Switzerland if we can help it. But if Father is really ill I promise I'll send for you."

Emmeline set off the same day and arrived in London the following day with only just enough time to catch the last train for Manchester. A man came into the railway carriage carrying an evening paper, and Emmeline noticed that the front page was edged with black, a sign of mourning and respect for someone distinguished who had died. She leaned forward to read the news. To her horror she saw that the dead man was Richard Pankhurst, her own husband.

The rest of the journey passed like a bad dream. When Emmeline reached home in the early hours of the morning Sylvia was waiting up for her, together with Emmeline's sister Mary, who was now married, and the faithful Susan, who was also married with a home of her own but had hurried to the Pankhursts' house to give the family what help she could. Emmeline's two youngest children,

Adela, who was just twelve, and Harry, not yet eight, had long since fallen asleep.

In the long, sad days which followed Emmeline was a little comforted by the hundreds of messages and letters she received. Everyone spoke highly of the man who had gladly sacrificed so much of his time to the public good. As one of Manchester's leading citizens wrote to Emmeline, "Your sorrow is shared by thousands."

CHAPTER 5

Birth of a New Movement

"FAITHFUL and true and my loving comrade!" Emmeline chose these words by the American writer Walt Whitman to inscribe on the headstone of her husband's grave. She missed him almost unbearably, but she could not give way to unhappiness, for she had to think of the children's future. Adela and Harry were at school; Sylvia, like her Aunt Mary, had a gift for painting and had just been awarded a scholarship at the Manchester School of Art; Christabel was still in Switzerland. Richard Pankhurst had died a poor man, and Emmeline knew she must find work so that she could support the children until they could fend for themselves.

The first thing she did was to move to a much smaller house. The problem of finding work was solved by the Chorlton Board of Guardians, which offered Emmeline the post of Registrar of Births and Deaths. The post carried a salary and the promise of a retirement pension, and Emmeline was thankful to accept it, although in doing so she had to resign her voluntary post as a Poor Law Guardian. As Registrar her hours of work were short, so she decided once again to open a shop, which she thought would eke out the family income and also provide work for Christabel when her year in Switzerland was up.

Her job meant that Emmeline was responsible for recording and returning to the office of the Registrar-General details of all the births and deaths which occurred in a large working-class district. The job brought her many new contacts and a fresh insight into the lives of the very poor. She was appalled by the tales of poverty and hardship she heard from women who came to her to record a birth or a death and were grateful to be able to unburden themselves to another woman. When she heard of wives with large families deserted by their husbands, of young, unmarried girls with babies of their own to support, her heart was heavy with anger against the men responsible for so much misery.

She had always known that women were considered of less account in the world than men, but the idea was borne in on her more strongly than ever when she was appointed a member of the Manchester School Board, which under the Board of Education was responsible for running the city's "Board"—or elementary— schools.

"It makes me burn with rage," she said, "when I hear of women teachers being paid so much less than men, when the women often have to teach sewing and domestic science as well as ordinary subjects without any extra pay."

Emmeline often spoke in this way, especially when she heard from the women teachers themselves of the inequality of their conditions. She knew that they even gave up part of their small salary to help pay for regular dinners for the children of unemployed parents, for local authorities had not at this time been given the power to feed hungry schoolchildren.

"You see," one of the teachers told Emmeline, "the little things are too badly off to study their lessons. We have to feed them before we can teach them."

She was also told that certain skilled jobs were closed to women, not because they were unfitted for the work but because the men feared that the employment of women would reduce the level of their own wages. For this reason, she learned, women were even barred from attending trade-school classes for professional cooks.

To Emmeline it was plain that there was no justice in a world in which women could not advance side by side with men. Women must be given political freedom, the right to vote for representatives in Parliament who would see that justice was given them. It seemed to her that the Socialists were more likely than the Conservatives or Liberals to fight for this equality. There were a number of supporters of women's suffrage in the Independent Labor Party, although the majority still thought of the vote as something to be gained for women in the distant future.

"Women must have the vote at once," said Emmeline, "and not in the future." Christabel, when she returned from Geneva, was as impatient as her mother.

Christabel had grown into a striking-looking young woman, with a wide, rosy-cheeked face, high cheekbones, and slightly slanting blue eyes. For her mother's sake she tried at first to make a success of the shop, but she soon found that she had no head for business and thoroughly disliked it. Sylvia, dreamy and artistic, was called on to take her turn in the shop, but she also hated it. Their mother, who did not want to drive them into doing anything they disliked, decided to close the shop down. Sylvia had her art, but Christabel, who had no particular bent, was at loose ends until her mother suggested that she should attend some classes at the university.

The idea appealed to Christabel, and in between lectures she went to political meetings. At these meetings she met members of the women's suffrage societies, women who were already working for the vote. When at question time she rose rather timidly to ask one of the speakers a question, she discovered that she enjoyed speaking and spoke clearly and well. One of the suffrage leaders told

Christabel Pankhurst

Emmeline that Christabel argued so well that she ought to be a lawyer.

When she heard this the girl decided that she would like to study law. She applied to become a law student at Lincoln's Inn, but her application, together with the applications of several other women, was refused. No one seemed willing to train women as lawyers. Instead, Christabel began a course at Manchester University leading to the Bachelor of Laws degree. She thought, and so did her mother, that a knowledge of law would be useful in the cause of women's suffrage.

Meanwhile, the Labor Party was moving far too slowly for the Pankhursts. The leader, Keir Hardie, the first

Sylvia Pankhurst

Socialist to be elected to Parliament, was all in favor of women being given the vote, but he could not carry all his supporters with him. When Socialist friends came to Mrs. Pankhurst's house, as they often did, they were surprised and a little annoyed to be bombarded with questions about their intentions by a very provocative Christabel.

"It's no use, Mother," said the girl after one of these visits. "If we rely on the Labor Party, women will never get the vote."

Emmeline sighed. "If all Socialists were like Mr. Keir Hardie we should get it soon enough. The trouble is that although they believe in the suffrage, when it comes to action they find that all sorts of other things come first."

Christabel's blue eyes glittered. "The idea of another generation of women wasting their lives just begging for the vote is quite unbearable. We mustn't lose any more time. We must act."

"You're right," said her mother excitedly, "we will act. As the Labor Party won't make the suffrage a party question we will form a women's organization and fight for it ourselves. If Labor will help us, so much the better. If not, we can fight alone."

Mother and daughter got to work at once. A few days later—on October 10, 1903—a litttle group of women met at Mrs. Pankhurst's house. In their Russell Square days the Pankhursts had had a vast double drawing room for meetings, and Emmeline had worn elegant evening dresses. The rooms in the Manchester house were small, and Emmeline had no money now for evening dress. The gathering was small, too, but the women who attended it were full of enthusiasm.

Emmeline, who took the chair, explained what she had in mind—an independent women's organization pledged to fight for the vote. Suffrage societies had existed for years, but they had gotten nowhere; something more effective was needed if women were ever to win the right to the vote.

When, as now, Emmeline was deeply moved her blue eyes flamed and the color came and went in her cheeks as it had as a girl. She looked delicate in comparison with her daughter, but there was a steely strength in her taut, upright figure, and a sincerity in her deep, expressive voice which no one could withstand.

"We shall demand immediate enfranchisement," declared Emmeline. "We want the vote now, and we mean to have it."

She called for a show of hands on the question of whether there should be a women's organization, and not a single woman voted against her.

After a good deal of discussion a name was chosen for the new organization. It was to be called the Women's Social and Political Union, or the W.S.P.U. for short.

"We need a rallying cry, too," said Emmeline. "Something really rousing. The old slogan, 'Women's Suffrage,' is too tame for us."

There was further talk, and then Emmeline herself found the right slogan. "Votes for Women," she cried passionately, and "Votes for Women" it became.

At first she was reluctant to take on the leadership of

the W.S.P.U. "We don't want people to think that our Union is simply a family party," she said, "just Mrs. Pankhurst and Christabel."

But although for the time being other officers were elected to run the Union, it was not long before the Pankhursts took over the leadership. Under their direction meeting were held every week, and new members were enrolled, who subscribed as much as they could afford to the Union's funds.

At first their work was confined to talks on women's suffrage to the women of Lancashire and Yorkshire, and most of their meetings were held under the wing of the Labor Party. W.S.P.U. members traveled from one town to another, speaking at trade union gatherings, debating societies, in parks and at street corners, at any place where they could be sure of an audience. Emmeline was far and away the best of speakers. People listened to her spellbound, carried away by the magic of her voice. Christabel, too, was exceedingly good, quick and very forceful in argument.

One of the first meetings was arranged by the Oldham Trades Council with Christabel as the speaker. The audience was disappointingly small, but after the meeting Christabel was approached by three eager recruits. They were sisters and their name was Kenney, said their spokesman, Annie, who had a long, intelligent face and a very determined chin.

Annie Kenney, who worked in an Oldham cotton factory, offered to arrange a meeting of her fellow workers if Christabel would talk to them. "I don't know much about organizing meetings," said Annie frankly, "but I'll do my best for you.'

Privately Christabel wondered if there would be anybody at the meeting at all except Annie and her two sisters; but the girl did her work well and the meeting she arranged, though small, was a great success. After this the two girls became firm friends. Almost every evening after work Annie would take the train from Oldham to Manchester and hurry to Mrs. Pankhurst's house to help in whatever work was going on.

It was Annie Kenney who suggested a new kind of audience. "Couldn't we try the Wakes?" she asked one evening as she sat at supper with Emmeline and Christabel.

Emmeline raised her fine dark eyebrows in surprise.

Annie Kenney

"The Wakes, Annie? Do you think the people would listen to us?"

The suggestion was a daring one. The Lancashire Wakes was a sort of traveling fair, with merry-go-rounds, entertainers and other sideshows, and covered booths where goods of all kinds were sold. Every village, even the smallest, had its Wakes Week in the summer or autumn, and the villagers always spent most of the Sunday before the opening wandering among the booths inspecting the goods.

"The people listen to the Salvation Army Speakers on that Sunday," said Annie, "and to temperance speakers as well as the men who sell quack medicines and such, so I don't see why they shouldn't listen to us."

"It's worth trying, Mother," said Christabel, and Emmeline agreed.

So W.S.P.U. speakers toured the Lancashire villages with the Wakes. At first no one took much notice of their suffrage speeches, but quite soon, as Emmeline noted, "we rivaled in popularity the Salvation Army, and even the tooth drawers and patent-medicine pedlars."

By this time the Kenney sisters had been joined by a number of other hard-working new members. They included Miss Theresa Billington, a Manchester elementary-school teacher with a very keen mind. Theresa Billington, strongly built, with a round face and a pleasing expression, was a tremendous asset, for she was a fine debater who could make short work of hecklers. A number of older women, members of the existing suffrage societies, also joined the W.S.P.U., but for the next two years it remained small and insignificant.

In February, 1905, however, Emmeline decided that the time had come to tackle Parliament. A women's suffrage measure had, in fact, been introduced into the House of Commons the previous year, but although it was well supported, it had been allowed to peter out. Emmeline did not expect the Government to do anything officially, but she hoped she could persuade a member of Parliament to sponsor women's suffrage on one of the Friday afternoons reserved for private members' bills. She therefore went to London to stay with Sylvia, who was living in Chelsea and studying at the Royal College of Art.

Keir Hardie, the square-faced, bearded Socialist leader, would gladly have helped, but he had drawn no place in the ballot which is always held to decide which of the many bills that members want to introduce shall be taken during the session. Twelve of the thirteen members who had been successful in the ballot were already pledged to other measures, but the thirteenth agreed to introduce a suffrage bill.

On the Friday afternoon on which it was to be taken quite a crowd of W.S.P.U. members—most of them from Manchester—assembled in the Outer Lobby of the House of Commons. Emmeline and one or two others had been given tickets for the Ladies' Gallery of the House, and their hopes were high when they took their seats. Their bill was the second on the list, the first being a bill to provide that, in view of the great increase in motor traffic, all horse-drawn carts should carry a rear light at night.

Emmeline waited with growing impatience to the droning arguments advanced on the floor of the House. She knew that if the House rose at the end of the day without the Suffrage Bill being taken, the longed-for measure would be abandoned. After a while her impatience gave way to suppressed fury, for she realized that certain members were deliberately prolonging their speeches. One member contrived to fill in half an hour by arguing that if a cart carried a rear light, then a horse should carry a red light on its tail, and an old washerwoman with a bundle of laundry should have a light on her back. These futile arguments were greeted with so many bursts of laughter that it soon became clear that certain members had banded together to make sure that the suffrage bill was "talked out," that is to say, there would be no time left to take it. And this is precisely what happened.

The W.S.P.U. members left the House dejectedly. They gathered around the statue of King Richard I, which stands near the House of Lords, to protest at the injustice of the situation. A police inspector came up and told them they must move on.

"And where can we go?" demanded Emmeline, her eyes blazing, her voice shaking with anger.

The inspector kindly led them to Broad Sanctuary near Westminster Abbey. There they were joined by Keir Hardie, who was as annoyed as they were about what had occurred. The women demanded, although they knew that they demanded in vain, that the Government should intervene to save the bill. Their little protest meeting passed almost unnoticed; yet it was the start of something really big.

CHAPTER 6

"We Are Not Satisfied!"

IN the autumn of the same year—1905—England was on the brink of a general election. The leaders of the Liberal Party expected to be returned to power after a long period of Conservative government. The W.S.P.U. decided to try and get an official statement from the leading Liberals as to whether, if they were returned to power, they would be in favor of women's suffrage.

An election meeting had been arranged at the Free Trade Hall, Manchester, at which the chief speaker was to be Sir Edward Grey, the man who was later to be Foreign Secretary. Also on the platform was the Liberal candidate for North-West Manchester, Mr. Winston Churchill, who had recently left the Conservatives and joined the Liberals.

The day of the meeting Christabel Pankhurst and Annie Kenney made a small white calico banner and painted on it in black furniture stain the words, "Votes for Women." They chattered excitedly as they worked, but Emmeline, who was listening, looked drawn and anxious. She knew that they planned to break the law; if they did, the responsibility would be hers.

"We shall sleep in prison tonight," said Christabel cheerfully as she said good-bye to her mother before she left for the meeting.

She and Annie were outwardly calm, but their hearts were thumping as they made their way to their seats, the furled banner tucked inside Christabel's coat. They planned to wait until the speeches were over before asking their question, in case Sir Edward Grey announced that the Liberal Party had already decided to put the suffrage question in their program.

He did not mention it, and so, at question time, Annie Kenney got to her feet to ask in her clear, North Country voice, "Will the Liberal Party, if returned, give votes to women?"

Sir Edward made no reply, whereupon Christabel rose to repeat the question, unfurling the banner as she spoke and holding it up for people to see. Again there was no reply. Instead, angry comment broke out in the hall against the two girls, and while the speakers on the platform consulted together, Christabel was roughly forced back into her seat by the men sitting nearest to her, one of whom pressed his hat over her face.

Christabel was a powerful girl. She struggled to her feet and repeated Annie's question, "Will the Liberal Party, if returned, give votes to women?"

There was still no answer, but the Chief Constable of Manchester stepped down from the platform and assured the girls that a reply would be given if they would wait quietly until the vote of thanks to the speaker had been proposed.

They waited. The vote of thanks was proposed; it was seconded by Mr. Churchill; and Sir Edward Grey then replied very briefly. He did not even mention the girls' question, and the meeting began to dissolve.

This was too much. Annie Kenney climbed onto her chair to shout the question above the sounds of talking and shuffling feet. At once a band of stewards bore down on the girls, dragged them into the center aisle and down the hall toward the platform. As they came level with the platform Christabel, using all her strength, managed to stand for a moment directly below Sir Edward Grey. Looking up at him she called out for the last time, "Will the Liberal Party, if returned, give women the vote?"

Although Sir Edward made no sign that he had heard, Christabel noticed that he looked very pale. Then she and Annie, resisting as hard as they could, were dragged through a side door and out into the street, where they were received by a party of policemen.

There was quite a number of people in the street who had just left the meeting, and Christabel and Annie started to address them. Christabel knew perfectly well that she could not be sent to prison for disturbing a meeting or talking to a crowd in the street; but she was absolutely determined to go to prison because she thought that this was the only way to draw attention to the fact that the women's suffrage question had simply been ignored—as she had guessed all along that it would be. In order to go to prison she must break the law and get herself arrested, and the quickest way to get herself arrested was to assault a policeman. But this was easier said than done. She raised her hand to strike, and her arms were immediately pinioned behind her; and she soon found that a policeman is very clever at keeping his feet out of the way of a girl who means to stamp on them. There was one other way of assaulting a policeman, however. Christabel drew her lips together in a pout and tried—quite unsuccessfully—to spit.

This was enough for the police. They arrested the two girls and dragged them, struggling and shouting, to the police station.

"What would your father have said to this?" demanded a policeman who had known Dr. Pankhurst and recognized his daughter.

Christabel refused to answer, but privately she thought he would have been very proud.

"This is what they've been aiming at," said another policeman. "All they want is some free publicity, and that's what they're going to get."

At the police station the girls were ordered to appear next morning at the police court to be charged. They went to Mrs. Pankhurst's home for the night, and Emmeline accompanied them to the court next morning. They were sentenced to pay a small fine, with the alternative of a few days in prison. Both unhesitatingly chose prison.

As soon as the case was over Emmeline rushed around to the room where the girls were waiting to be taken to prison. "I think now," she said, "you should let me pay your fines and take you home."

Christabel drew herself up. "If you pay my fine, Mother," she said defiantly, "I shall never go home."

Emmeline gave way. She knew in her heart that nothing she could say would move her stubborn daughter, and where Christabel led Annie Kenney would follow. Emmeline knew that the real leadership was hers, that she alone could lead the suffragettes into action. The knowledge may have scared her a little, but it also stimulated her. She had no personal ambtion, but she had found a cause to which she could devote herself heart and soul. She was sure that her husband would have been glad for her to be the suffragette leader, and this made the cause seem all the more important.

To the two girls, going to prison was something of an adventure, but it was an uncomfortable one. They had to wear old-fashioned prison clothes, heavy with pleats and exceedingly rough to the skin, and ugly caps on their heads. They were put in separate boxlike cells, each having a tiny window set high in the wall. The only furniture was a wooden stool, a shelf which did duty as a table, a plank for a bed, and a straw mattress, which was rolled up during the day. The prisoners ate with wooden spoons from battered tins; their food consisted of a sort of porridge for breakfast, a thin broth with small pieces of meat floating in it for the midday meal, with dark bread, and, to drink, watery tea or cocoa. They were let out of their cells only twice a day, once for an hour's exercise march in single file around and around the prison yard, and once for chapel, where Christabel and Annie sat side by side.

Had they wished, the girls could have ended their imprisonment at any moment. More than one sympathizer called at the prison and offered to pay their fines. Indeed, there was rumor that Mr. Churchill himself had offered to pay, for he was known to be in favor of giving women the vote, and had voted in favor of it in 1904.

Beyond the prison walls the affair was creating quite a sensation, but Emmeline, scanning the newspapers, noted bitterly that almost all the comment was critical.

"If any argument were required against giving ladies political status and power," declared a Birmingham paper, "it has been furnished in Manchester." Another paper insisted that fines and imprisonment were too good for such unwomanly creatures, "Our only regret is that the discipline will be identical with that experienced by mature and sensible women, and not that which falls to the lot of children in the nursery."

There were, however, plenty of people who wrote to the newspapers expressing their admiration for the brave stand the two girls had taken. When, very early in the morning, Christabel and Annie were released they found a crowd of strangers waiting to greet them. A very short woman, almost as broad as she was high, rushed forward to shake them by the hand. Her name, she told them, was Mrs. Flora Drummond, and she wished to join the Union and do all she could to help.

A demonstration of welcome had been arranged by Theresa Billington at the Free Trade Hall, from which the girls had been thrown out only the previous week. This time there were no ejections, and the triumphant ex-prisoners spoke confidently from the platform of the victory to come.

The imprisonment of Christabel and Annie was really

the start of the Union's long militant campaign to win the vote for women. Members now had a new name; the *Daily Mail* had christened them "suffragettes," and the name stuck.

Emmeline Pankhurst, now the undisputed leader of the suffragettes, began to press for more lively and sensational methods of drawing public attention to their cause. Suffragettes were news, as the publicity in the press on Christabel's imprisonment had shown. The thing to do was to follow up the publicity by every possible means. This suggestion made members of the older women's suffrage societies extremely uneasy. Their own methods were straightforward and sincere, and they detested cheap publicity.

The suffragettes were determined to go their own way —Mrs. Pankhurst's way—whatever other people might think. They waited until after the general election in December, 1905. The election brought a Liberal Government to power, but for the first time in its history Labor emerged as a force to be reckoned with.

Shortly after the formation of his Government the new Prime Minister, Sir Henry Campbell-Bannerman, went to the Royal Albert Hall to address a rally of his supporters. Annie Kenney, sitting demurely in one of the boxes, chose a quiet moment to ask in her clear, penetrating voice, "Will the Liberal Government give women the vote?" At the same moment the ex-schoolteacher, Theresa Billington, who was sitting high up in the seats behind the platform, let down a large white banner with the painted words, "Will the Liberal Government give justice to working women?"

Annie Kenney received no reply to her question, nor did she really expect one. Shouting and struggling she and Theresa Billington were marched out of Albert Hall.

This incident was quickly followed by others of the same kind, until not a single member of the Government was able to make a speech outside Parliament without interruption. From somewhere or other in the hall he would be questioned about his views on women's suffrage, while here and there white calico banners with their "Votes for Women" slogan would appear.

It was now that Christabel Pankhurst made up her mind that the campaign could not be carried on from Manchester.

"We must get down to work in London," she said.

Her mother was doubtful at first. There was something splendidly impulsive about her, a warmth which delighted her followers, but at this moment she was cautious. "I don't see how we can afford it," she said. "I've put every penny I possess into the movement already. Here in Manchester we can work on a shoestring, but in London we should need offices and staff, and where is the money to come from?"

"The money will come," answered Christabel confidently. "We simply can't allow the Government to escape us, and the only way to attack the Government is in Parliament."

Emmeline nodded slowly. She was as eager as her daughter to carry on the fight from London, but she could see the difficulties which Christabel ignored. "We must be practical," she said at last. "We can't afford failure. If we fail we're finished."

"By all means let's be practical," said Christabel. "How much money have we left in our election fund?"

"Most of it went in helping Keir Hardie to keep his seat. There is exactly two pounds left."

"That will do for a beginning, Mother. Annie Kenney will go on ahead and start rousing London. If we hadn't got two pounds she'd manage on two pence."

Suddenly it all seemed right to Emmeline, right and inevitable. In the future people would sometimes say that Mrs. Pankhurst, who would take orders from nobody, allowed her eldest daughter to influence her. Certainly Christabel influenced her now. If she had not done so, the suffragette story might have ended differently.

"Very well," said Emmeline, her mind made up. "Annie shall go to London, but you must stay in Manchester until you've taken your law degree. Annie can share Sylvia's rooms in Chelsea, and I will join them if I can find someone else to do my Registrar's work while I'm away."

The Board of Guardians gave Emmeline permission to go away if she could find someone to take her place. Her deputy was her own sister Mary, whose marriage had not been a happy one and who was glad to take on Emmeline's work.

It took a fortnight for the arrangements to be made, and when Emmeline reached London, she found that Annie had been exceedingly busy. Annie and Sylvia together had organized a procession of women to march from Caxton Hall to the Houses of Parliament for the opening of Parliament in February, 1906. There was to be a meeting at Caxton Hall first, and Keir Hardie had managed to raise the money to rent the hall and cover other expenses.

The day of the opening of Parliament was cold and wet, yet four hundred women marched to Caxton Hall from the East End of London. The hall was already well filled when they arrived, and waiting for them on the platform were Emmeline Pankhurst, Annie Kenney, and round little Flora Drummond, who had been so anxious to be present that she had borrowed the price of her fare from Manchester.

Emmeline spoke to the assembled women of her determination to fight for the vote until it was won. Her audience thrilled to the beauty of her voice. Then Annie Kenney spoke; she was still speaking when news was brought to the platform that in Parliament the King's Speech had been read. The Speech promised the vote to many men who did not yet possess it, but not a word was said about votes for women.

When the news had been read to the meeting Emmeline came down from the platform to lead her followers out of the hall into the driving rain. The procession was to march to the House of Commons and there urge members of Parliament to introduce a bill which would give women the vote. The women were expected, and they reached the Houses of Parliament to find the Strangers' Entrance closed and guarded by police.

Inside the House, Keir Hardie, replying to the King's

Speech as leader of the Labor Party, demanded that the "scandal and disgrace" of treating women as though they had no more rights than criminals or the insane should be removed. Keir Hardie's speech aroused a good deal of sympathy, but his party as a whole was not behind him.

After a good deal of argument the Speaker, who had at first refused to allow the women to be admitted to the House, agreed that they should enter twenty at a time. This was done, and for hours hundreds of women patiently waited their turn in the cold and wet. Some never got into the House at all; those who did were promised nothing. But they had made their protest, and that was something, however little.

After this disappointment Emmeline decided that more drastic and widespread measures were required. People of influence in public life were needed for this new campaign, besides far more money than the W.S.P.U. possessed. Keir Hardie provided the solutions to both problems when he introduced Emmeline to his friends, Mr. Pethick-Lawrence and his wife, whose name was also Emmeline and who was a few years younger than Mrs. Pankhurst.

Mr. Pethick-Lawrence, who belonged to a wealthy London family, had been educated at Eton and Cambridge University, where he had been president of the Union, the famous debating society whose presidents often make their mark afterward in politics. He was a barrister, and also exceedingly interested in social work—and so was his wife. The Pethick-Lawrences were already keen supporters of women's suffrage. When they met Emmeline Pankhurst, Mrs. Pethick-Lawrence accepted the post of honorary treasurer of the W.S.P.U., while her husband gave most generous sums of money from his own pocket and also helped the W.S.P.U. with his advice and by raising large additional funds. Together husband and wife founded and edited the W.S.P.U.'s paper, *Votes for Women;* for the next six years Emmeline Pankhurst had their willing help and support.

The fight which started in 1906 needed plenty of courage. It was not easy for women who had led very sheltered lives to make themselves unpopular and ridiculous to their friends by interrupting meetings and scuffling in a painful, undignified way with the police. But, where Christabel Pankhurst and Annie Kenney had led the way, others now followed. Some, like Flora Drummond, enjoyed it, but others found it very hard at first.

It was clear that the suffragettes would not be able to work happily with members of the older suffrage societies. These were now led by Mrs. Millicent Fawcett, a great educational worker and one of the founders of Newnham, the Cambridge college for women. Mrs. Fawcett and her supporters—who numbered men as well as women—had all this time been carrying on their own campaign. They held meetings all over the country, and these meetings were always held in an orderly way. The suffragists had no intention of giving up the fight until the vote was won. But they would fight only by strictly lawful means; assaulting the police and getting sent to prison was certainly not in their program.

At this time the suffragist organizations, grouped together as the National Union of Women's Suffrage Societies, were busy organizing a delegation to the Prime Minister, Sir Henry Campbell-Bannerman, to ask for the Government's support in their cause. They knew that the Prime Minister would receive their group. They were very annoyed to hear that the sensational suffragettes, whose new methods they thoroughly disliked, had already tried to do the same thing. The suffragettes had been led by Flora Drummond, whose leadership powers were to earn her the title of "General." The suffragettes had stood on

Mrs. Fawcett, leader of the law-abiding constitutional suffragists

the doorstep of No. 10 Downing Street demanding that the Prime Minister should receive them. When no attention was paid to them, the General pressed a knob which she thought was a bell. The knob opened the door, and the General, with Annie Kenney close behind her, rushed into the house in search of the Cabinet room. They had nearly reached it before they were caught and turned back; but although they were arrested, they were not prosecuted.

If the suffragists were annoyed by the General's behavior, they were still more annoyed by a scene which occurred soon afterward, in May, 1906. Keir Hardie had at length won a place in the ballot for private members' bills and was to introduce a women's suffrage measure. Several members of the National Union of Women's Suffrage Societies, of which Mrs. Fawcett was president, were present in the Ladies' Gallery of the House of Commons to listen to the debate. As they took their places behind the heavy grill which screened the gallery from the floor of the House, their hearts must have sunk to see Emmeline Pankhurst and some of her hot-headed friends already in place. Emmeline was afraid that the measure would be talked out, like the previous year's bill, and she was taking no chances.

No party line was to be taken. That is to say, members would be free to vote as they wished and would not be expected to vote as members of the Conservative, Liberal or Labor Parties.

The debate began with a long speech by a Mr. M. Cremer, who was out to destroy the measure by sneering at it.

"Are honorable members prepared," he asked, "to hand over the government of the country to women, the majority of whom are not breadwinners, and who have not to bear the burdens, and who do not understand the responsibilities of life? I am sometimes described in regard to this question as a woman-hater, but I have had two wives, and I think that this is the best answer I can give to those who call me a woman-hater." Women, went on Mr. Cremer, were impulsive, superficial creatures who were bored by politics and would never understand them. If women were given the vote they would at the same time be given a responsibility which they could not be expected to use wisely.

Mr. Cremer went on speaking for a long time, and on the floor of the House an angry murmur could be heard coming from the direction of the Ladies' Gallery. The Speaker, seated below the gallery, sent a message to the police to be ready to clear it if the disturbance did not cease. It did cease, and the debate continued. It was getting late when Mr. Samuel Evans, the member who had talked out the previous bill, rose with a grin and a look toward the clock. If he could prolong his speech until eleven o'clock there would be no time to take a vote and he would therefore have talked out Keir Hardie's measure.

Expecting trouble, the police began to gather at the back of the gallery. The suffragettes saw the police and craned eagerly in Mrs. Pankhurst's direction for a signal she had promised to give if events went against them. She gave the signal. Her followers started to protest loudly.

"Divide, divide!" shouted a suffragette, copying Parliamentary procedure.

Startled, members looked up at the gallery, to see a host of little white "Votes for Women" banners which had been pushed through the openings of the grill.

The police promptly seized the demonstrators and dragged them out of the gallery. Below, the House rose to a good deal of indignant comment. Keir Hardie's measure was lost.

The suffragettes met downstairs in the lobby. With them were a number of law-abiding suffragists, coldly angry at the scene that had taken place.

"If you had waited," said one of them, "we might have had a friendly speech from the Prime Minister."

"Mr. Evans was not going to give the Prime Minister or anyone else time to speak," answered Emmeline.

"Mr. Cremer called women impulsive creatures who don't know how to take responsibility," said another suffragist. "Judging by your behavior this evening he wasn't far short of the truth."

Emmeline faced her critics coolly and spoke with disdain of women who had not the courage to protest against injustice. If she felt any doubt about the wisdom of the protest at such a time she did not show it. Then Keir Hardie appeared in the lobby and hurried to her side. The sneers of members like Mr. Cremer and Mr. Evans, he assured her, and the action of the police entirely justified the disturbance.

But few people agreed with Keir Hardie. It looked at first as though the W.S.P.U. was not to be allowed to take part in the delegation to the Prime Minister which the National Union of Women's Suffrage Societies was organizing. But their faithful Socialist friend, Keir Hardie, was able to arrange for the suffragettes to be represented with Emmeline Pankhurst as their chief representative.

The leader of the whole group was Emily Davies, who had spent many years campaigning for women's rights, particularly in the fight to provide good schools for girls. The delegation was not a large one, but it represented 260,000 women of all kinds—university graduates, textile workers, trade unionists, and so on. Also present were members of Parliament belonging to the three political parties.

The Prime Minister received the delegation with politeness, and he listened gravely to what the leaders had to say.

When it came to Emmeline's turn to speak for the W.S.P.U. she addressed him with deep feeling. "We feel this question so keenly," she said, "that we are prepared to sacrifice for it life itself, or what is perhaps even harder, the means by which we live."

She might have been thinking of herself as she spoke, for she was now so seldom in Manchester that she was in danger of losing her job as Registrar. Her children's future, too, was unsettled. Christabel had just taken her degree; she and Sylvia were working for the W.S.P.U., but neither of them had a settled job in view. Adela, Emmeline's third daughter, had a teaching post in an elementary school, but she had decided to throw it up to work for the Union. Harry, the youngest, was a delicate boy of fifteen who lived at home in the care of his Aunt Mary.

The children's future would settle itself, thought Emmeline, once the vote had been won. But now, listening to the Prime Minister, she realized that the day was still far off.

Sir Henry Campbell-Bannerman was assuring the delegation that he himself was in favor of giving women the vote. He agreed with all the arguments they put forward, but he did not propose to do anything about them. Indeed, he could not, for the Cabinet and the Liberal Party were divided on the subject. All he could do was to advise everybody to be patient. He also suggested that they should go on pestering so that their demands should not be forgotten.

The Prime Minister was answered by Keir Hardie. "Patience can be carried to excess," he said bitterly. "Since both Liberal and Conservative leaders are agreed, and I know I speak for Mr. Balfour, the former Conservative Prime Minister, as well as for you, sir, and for myself as leader of the Labor Party, it surely does not pass the wit of statesmen to find ways and means to enfranchise the women of England before this Parliament comes to a close."

Sir Henry did not reply. He simply shook his head.

This response enraged Annie Kenney, who was standing close to Emmeline. She leaped onto a chair so that everybody could see her, shouting, "Sir, we are not satisfied!"

Annie did not expect an answer, nor did she receive one. But the suffragettes took one remark of the Prime

Minister's very much to heart. He had suggested that they should go on pestering, and while they had very little patience, they were full of ideas on the best way to pester the Government.

Before they dispersed they reminded one another that they would meet again the same day in Trafalgar Square. By three o'clock in the afternoon seven thousand people had gathered in the square. On the wide plinth beneath the immensely tall column on which stands the statue of Nelson, the suffragette leaders gathered between two of the four crouching lions which guard the column. Emmeline was there, dressed quietly and plainly with a fur stole about her shoulders and a quilled hat set far enough back on her head for her calm face to be clearly seen. On her left was her oldest supporter, Mrs. Wolstenholme Elmy, seventy-two years of age, a tiny woman dressed in black with a black bonnet on her long gray curls. Theresa Billington was there too, wearing bright blue; and Annie Kenney, dressed in the clothes she wore in the cotton mill—clogs, a white blouse, dark blue skirt, and a gray shawl over her hair, which hung in a long braid down her back. With them were Keir Hardie and other sympathizers, men as well as women. Emmeline, Annie Kenney, Keir Hardie, Theresa Billington, and Mrs. Elmy spoke of their fixed intention never to rest until the fight was won, and no one listening to them that afternoon can have doubted that they meant what they said.

CHAPTER 7

How to Be Militant

After the delegation to the Prime Minister and the Trafalgar Square meeting the rift between the suffragettes and the suffragists began to widen. Under Mrs. Fawcett's strong, steady leadership the National Union of Women's Suffrage Societies was gaining recruits all over the country. Although Mrs. Fawcett was President, the Union was run democratically, largely through its own local branches.

The W.S.P.U., on the other hand, was not a democratic body; it was controlled entirely by Emmeline Pankhurst and the Pethick-Lawrences, and later by Christabel. Their word was law, and every decision came from them. "Deeds not words" became their motto. While the National Union ran orderly meetings and sent delegations, the deeds of the W.S.P.U. were growing more daring and spectacular. Interruptions at political meetings went on continuously. Cabinet Ministers were heckled wherever they appeared, the particular target being Mr. Asquith, who was Chancellor of the Exchequer and was soon to become Liberal Prime Minister.

In the summer of 1906 Emmeline and other members

of the W.S.P.U. went to Nottingham, where Mr. Asquith was due to speak on the Government's education policy. They expected to be thrown out of the meeting for they had every intention of questioning the Chancellor. However, the president of the local Women's Liberal Association assured Emmeline that this would not be so.

"What happens in other cities," she said, "could not happen in Nottingham. You will be given a fair hearing, I promise you."

Emmeline was not in the hall when the meeting opened. Instead, she was holding a suffrage meeting of her own outside the building. She had scarcely begun to speak when several suffragettes were flung out of the hall. From their disheveled looks they had obviously been violently handled.

"We tried to question Mr. Asquith before he began his speech," said one of them, "and we were simply bundled out of the place."

"So much for the president's promise," said Emmeline grimly. "You will take charge of this meeting and I will take your place inside."

Looking cool and composed, Emmeline slipped into the hall. She found a seat in the front row, which had been reserved for prominent women supporters of the Liberal Party, and sat there in silence, noting that each time a man in the audience interrupted the speaker he was given a fair hearing and an answer to his questions.

When Mr. Asquith had finished his speech, Emmeline stood up. "Mr. Chairman," she said, in her quiet but penetrating voice, "I should like to ask Mr. Asquith a question about education."

The Chairman turned inquiringly to Mr. Asquith, who frowned and shook his head.

Emmeline disregarded the warning. "Mr. Asquith," she went on, "has said that the parents of children have a right to be consulted in the matter of their children's education, especially on such questions as the kind of religious instruction they should receive. Women are parents. Does not Mr. Asquith think that women should have the right to control their children's education, as men do, through the vote?"

The question remain unanswered. But Emmeline was seized by a pair of hefty stewards, who rushed her to the door and ran her out of the building.

Afterward the president of the Women's Association came to find her.

"I was promised faithfully that this would not happen, Mrs. Pankhurst," she said in great distress. "Please accept my deep apologies."

"I'm sure you spoke in good faith," answered Emmeline, "but I'm not so trusting as you are. Believe me, I was neither surprised nor disappointed to be thrown out."

"You must tell me more about your movement," said the other woman. "I'm so disgusted by what has taken place that I have decided to resign from my job as president. Instead, if you will have me, I shall join the W.S.P.U."

"Of course we'll have you," said Emmeline. "You are just the kind of recruit we need."

Fresh plans were being worked out the whole time. It was clear to Emmeline now that a certain amount of disguise was necessary. Her followers must not look like troublemakers or they would be thrown out even before they began to speak. But nobody would suspect a stately dowager, grandly dressed in black, with furs, a large, feathered hat, and a veil fashionably covering her face from forehead to chin and tied at the nape of her neck. Nobody would suspect an unobtrusive, meek-looking woman either; instructions were given out about dress and behavior.

There were lessons in heckling as well.

"Sooner or later," said Emmeline to her followers, "you'll get your chance. Now, I'll be the speaker, and you interrupt me." She drew herself up and spoke in a booming, platform voice. "One great question remains to be settled . . ."

She paused. "Go on, one of you, interrupt me. I'll repeat what I said. 'One great question remains to be settled.' "

"And that is women's suffrage," ventured someone.

"Good," cried Emmeline in her own voice. "That's the idea." She boomed again, "Under the circumstances we must . . ."

"Give votes to women."

"Splendid! You just need a little practice and you'll all be expert hecklers." She smiled. "And you'll have plenty of opportunities for being flung out of meetings."

In the autumn of the same year they opened a London headquarters. This was in Clement's Inn, off the Strand, where the Pethick-Lawrences lived. The office was manned by volunteers, including the General, who pounded away at her own typewriter which she had brought with her from Manchester, and Annie Kenney's sister Jessie, who was very slim and boyish-looking; sometimes she was disguised as a messenger boy.

The day Parliament reopened in October, Emmeline led a group into the lobby of the House of Commons. Through the Chief Liberal Whip she sent a message to Sir Henry Campbell-Bannerman.

"Does the Prime Minister hold out any hope for women's suffrage during this Parliament or at any future time?" she asked.

Office of the W.S.P.U.

"No, Mrs. Pankhurst," was the reply, "the Prime Minister does not."

At this, several suffragettes jumped up and began to protest, one after the other.

The police intervened, and in the struggle which followed Emmeline was flung to the ground. Ten women got themselves arrested, among them Emmeline's youngest daughter Adela, Emmeline Pethick-Lawrence, Annie Kenney, and Theresa Billington. They were all sent to prison for six weeks, while Sylvia Pankhurst, who tried to make a speech of protest from the steps of the police court, was sentenced to a fortnight's imprisonment.

Being sent to prison made the suffragettes martyrs for their cause, and well they knew it. Now that the Liberal Government had definitely shown its hand, the W.S.P.U. became an enemy of the Liberals. Whenever a by-election campaign took place suffragettes were in the borough with the object of dissuading as many people as possible from voting for the Liberal candidate. Suffragettes who had already been to prison could back up their appeal with stories of the harsh prison life to which a Liberal Government had condemned them, their only crime being that they demanded the right to vote. These stories gained many new recruits for the movement, and more and more women declared themselves ready to go to prison for their rights.

The by-election campaigns were a nuisance to the Government although it was hard to tell how much effect the suffragettes had on the results.

The suffragettes became even more of a nuisance early

the following year when Emmeline called a parliament of her own. The Women's Parliament met at Caxton Hall in Westminster in February, 1907, to discuss the King's Speech to Parliament which had been delivered the previous day, and which—not surprisingly—had contained no reference to the question of women's suffrage.

Emmeline was in the chair. Amid scenes of tremendous enthusiasm, the meeting passed a resolution calling on the Government to provide an opportunity for women's suffrage to be debated.

At the back of the platform a banner was unfurled bearing the words, "Rise up, women!" And from the body of the hall came the answering cry, "Now!"

"We must be ready for Parliament or prison," Emmeline warned the volunteers who clamored for the privilege of carrying the resolution to the House of Commons.

They would allow nothing to deter them, and a delegation was chosen which was to be led by Mrs. Despard, an elderly woman who had spent many years working for the poor of South London. Mrs. Despard was an elder sister of Field Marshal Sir John French, who was later to command the British Forces in France at the beginning of the First World War. She was most dignified and striking-looking, for on her piled-up white hair she always wore a black lace veil like a Spanish mantilla.

The other members of the group followed Mrs. Despard into the gathering dusk of the cold February afternoon. Behind them marched many of the women who had attended the Women's Parliament. They had reached Parliament Square when they found their way to the

Houses of Parliament blocked by a solid body of police. Orders had been given to the police that the women must not be allowed to pass. They may have hoped that the women would turn tamely back; if they did they were disappointed, for the suffragette army pressed forward. As they came up to the waiting policemen the women were seized by the arms, swung around and pummeled between the shoulders and bumped in the back. Some of them were pushed straight in the path of a body of mounted police. They staggered and fell to the ground,

Mrs. Despard

while the police reared their well-trained horses over them.

It was a terrifying ordeal, but the women stood it bravely. All through the early hours of the evening they battled to break through the police line. Every now and then some of them went back to Caxton Hall for a short rest. Their clothes were torn, their hats had gone, their faces were grimy, and their hair streamed down their backs; yet, after a brief respite, they sallied forth again to continue the fight. A few actually succeeded in forcing their way into the precincts of the House of Commons. There they started to hold a protest meeting, and the police promptly arrested them. More arrests were made in Parliament Square, and the next day more than fifty women —and two men—appeared in the police court. Among them were the elderly Mrs. Despard and the Pankhurst girls, Christabel and Sylvia.

Christabel's case was the first to be heard by the magistrate. She looked young and innocent with her rosy cheeks, but her head was high and there was a dangerous spark in her eyes.

Her crime, she was told, was obstructing the police in the exercise of their duty.

"There was no obstruction," said Christabel in a clear, confident voice. "Our delegation was a perfectly peaceful attempt to present a resolution to the Prime Minister. As we have no vote we cannot elect members of Parliament who will plead our cause for us; we had no alternative but to try and present our resolution."

The magistrate looked at her sternly. "These disorderly scenes must be stopped," he said.

"I quite agree with you," replied Christabel sweetly. "But that doesn't depend on us, it depends on the Government. Sooner or later the Government will have to accept our resolution and give us our right. There will be no going back for us, and a great deal will happen if we do not get the vote."

"Twenty shillings or fourteen days," snapped the magistrate, ignoring Christabel's speech.

The girl chose to go to prison, and so did many of the other defendants, including Mrs. Despard and Sylvia Pankhurst.

A week or so later a private member's bill was introduced, which aimed at giving the vote to women of means. The bill was talked out, as everybody had known it would be.

At nearby Caxton Hall another meeting of the Women's Parliament was held, and a second group set out for the Houses of Parliament. In the struggle which followed with the police seventy-five women were arrested and charged with obstruction. Three of them received heavier sentences than the others—thirty days' imprisonment. This was because for two of the three it was a second offense—they had been sent to prison after the last fight with the police; the third—Mrs. Mary Leigh—had added to her offense by audaciously hanging a "Votes for Women" banner over the witness box while she was being charged.

Emmeline Pankhurst did not lead the group herself, for she was not in London at the time but away organizing her forces in another by-election campaign. Because of her suffrage work and the publicity it was given in the newspapers, she had been dismissed from her post as Registrar of Births and Deaths. If she had agreed to give up her suffrage activities, she could have kept her post and earned her pension, but this she would not do. She was free now to go from one by-election to another, and nineteen took place in a single year. Whenever a Liberal candidate was defeated or returned to Parliament with a reduced majority the suffragettes were triumphant. Naturally, their campaign made them even less popular with the Government than they had been before.

It had already been decided at W.S.P.U. headquarters that no member should support any political party until women were given the vote. Emmeline had resigned from the Labor Party several years earlier. Now the Pethick-Lawrences and other well-known Socialists followed suit.

The Pethick-Lawrences were completely in charge of the Union's money affairs. They were wonderful fund-raisers. Thanks to their skill there was always money to continue the fight, to provide salaries for the paid workers, and to enable Emmeline herself to live without an income. Emmeline was as economical as she possibly could be. Although she was fond of good clothes and fine materials, she now spent practically nothing on herself; every penny that could be spared must go to the cause. She was still a beautiful woman, with a voice and a smile of immense charm. If she no longer wore the elegant evening gowns which her daughters remembered from their childhood, she could fascinate her audience just as easily in a plain dark dress or suit.

Every week she held an informal reception at Queen's

Hall. At these receptions Emmeline welcomed new members and praised old friends. She spoke from the platform of the spirit of the movement, which was both serious and happy, and of its keynote—loyalty to the cause and to its leaders.

"Courage comes next to loyalty," Emmeline told her followers on one occasion. "By courage I don't mean simply physical courage, although many of you have already shown physical courage most splendidly. I mean still more the moral courage which helps us to endure misunderstanding, ridicule, and unjust criticism."

When she spoke, simply and quietly and with a note of sadness in her voice, of loyalty and courage most of her hearers resolved to follow her to the death. But there were some who were worried by this insistence on absolute loyalty to their leaders. They found Emmeline something of a dictator, and were annoyed because the rank-and-file had no say at all in running the movement. Emmeline, the Pethick-Lawrences, and now Christabel also, were the leaders. Their critics admired and respected them; but, like other leaders, they might sometimes be wrong, and, in any event, it was never right to demand blind, unquestioning obedience.

Nevertheless, Emmeline did demand blind obedience, and from all except the little band of critics she received it. In due course the critics—led by the elderly Mrs. Despard and by Theresa Billington, who by now had married and was Mrs. Billington-Greig—broke away from the W.S.P.U. and founded their own Women's Freedom League. Like the W.S.P.U., the Women's Freedom League fought for women's suffrage by violent, militant means; in this it was unlike the National Union of Women's Suffrage Societies, whose members continued to work in an orderly, lawful manner.

Mrs. Pethick-Lawrence (left) and Christabel Pankhurst

Within the ranks of the W.S.P.U. there was no longer anyone who disputed Emmeline's leadership. Although officially she shared the leadership with the Pethick-Lawrences and her own daughter, she was really the guiding spirit. There were two reasons for this. The first was because the movement owed its existence and growing strength largely to her. The second was her own personality. Many suffragettes felt for Emmeline Pankhurst the sort of crush which schoolgirls sometimes feel for older girls or teachers. They hero-worshiped her, and as was only natural, she responded to the affection and admiration which placed her on a pedestal high above them. She had only to give an order and a hundred women would rush to obey without thought or question. In the years to come she would drive her supporters hard, but because they loved her and knew that she was prepared to share their sufferings, many of them endured far more than they would have with another leader.

CHAPTER 8

Emmeline Goes to Prison

So far, although others had been to prison, Emmleine had not. Early in 1908, however, she decided that the time for her own imprisonment had come. She therefore came to London after the last of a series of by-election fights. One of them—in Devonshire—had resulted in an unexpected defeat for the Liberal candidate. After the declaration of the poll a band of hooligans wearing the Liberal colors seized hold of Emmeline, yelling, "Those women did it." They threw her down on the muddy ground and, but for the intervention of the police, would have thrust her into a barrel and rolled her down the street.

She emerged from this encounter bruised and limping from a badly sprained ankle, and arrived in London just in time to take the chair at a meeting of the Women's Parliament. The usual resolution was passed demanding votes for women, and volunteers were called for to carry the resolution to the Houses of Parliament.

There was never any lack of volunteers, but before they were chosen Emmeline rose to speak. She looked white and drawn, for her injured foot was giving her a good deal of pain, but her voice was clear and confident. "I feel," she said, "that the time has come when I must act, and I wish to be one of those to carry our resolution to Parliament this afternoon."

There was an immediate outcry from the body of the hall. "Mrs. Pankhurst must not go. . . . We cannot spare our leader!"

"If you can be spared to go to prison," said Emmeline calmly when the hubbub had died down, "then so can I."

Cheers broke out all over the hall as twelve other women were chosen to follow her. One of them was the stout little General; another was the fearless, firm-chinned Annie Kenney.

Emmeline hobbled down the steps of Caxton Hall and limped into the street as a two-wheeled cart was driven by.

The General called out to the driver, "Will you take Mrs. Pankhurst to the House of Commons?"

The man reined in his horse. "Jump up, lady," he cried obligingly.

Emmeline was helped up beside him. He drove off at a walking pace, and the group marched in twos behind the cart.

"That lot won't get far," sneered a bystander.

He was right, for the cart had scarcely started before a policeman appeared at the horse's head. He ordered the passenger to dismount and the group to march in single file.

Emmeline got down from her perch and set out again at the head of her little procession. A crowd had already gathered in Parliament Square to watch the fun, and the route was lined with policemen.

Walking on her swollen ankle made Emmeline feel faint and so she paused to ask if two of the women would help her along. They did so, and she struggled on, arm in arm with her two supporters.

She had not gone more than a few steps when a couple of policemen barred her way.

The "General"—Mrs. Drummond

"You were ordered to walk in single file," said one of them. "Mrs. Pankhurst, you are under arrest." He pushed aside her companions and grasped her by the elbow.

There was a brief struggle, and then the two women and five others, including Annie Kenney, were also arrested.

The seven of them were released on bail for the night, and they all took part in the evening session of the Women's Parliament.

The audience cheered and shouted their welcome and the speeches were punctuated with long bursts of applause.

"We shall never rest or falter," declared Emmeline, "till the long, weary struggle for enfranchisement is won." She guessed that the struggle would be lengthy and bitter, but she did not know how desperate it was soon to become.

The next morning Emmeline appeared with the other women at Westminster police court. She was given the choice of being bound over for twelve months' good behavior or going to prison for six months. Naturally, she would give no undertaking to refrain from protests or disturbances for a whole year and so she chose prison.

The prisoners were taken to Holloway and, after a long wait in an icy-cold reception room, they were led to a large room where they had to strip and allow themselves to be searched. Their own clothes and belongings were taken away and they were ordered to dress in prison clothes. It made Emmeline feel really ill to have to put on the patched, stained prison underwear; the badly darned, harsh wool stockings, brown with red stripes, which kept falling down to her ankles because there was nothing to hold them up; the three clumsy petticoats;

and the coarse dress tied with tapes and stamped all over with broad arrows. The arrows were the prison sign, known to everybody, so that if ever a prisoner succeeded in escaping she would be recognized at once.

When they had dressed the prisoners were locked separately in their cold but stuffy cells. Emmeline tossed and turned all night on her hard plank bed, tormented by worrying thoughts. She remembered the happy years of her marriage as though they belonged to a different life, when everything had seemed safe and the future peaceful. She fretted about her children, especially about the girls, whose futures were now bound up with hers. Many of her old friends disapproved of what she was doing, and not so long ago she had had a stinging letter from her old school friend Noémie telling her that she ought to leave politics alone and find suitable professions for her daughters. Harry, her delicate only son, was also a worry. He was now apprenticed to a builder in Glasgow and unhappy in the work, which was chiefly concerned with putting up barracklike dwellings for the working classes.

Yet, worried as she was, Emmeline had no thought of turning back. She had committed herself to the cause, whatever suffering it might bring. And, to a woman who was neither young nor strong, prison life brought plenty of suffering. The prisoners were kept in solitary confinement except in chapel and during the exercise hour in the bitterly cold yard, where they were not allowed to speak. After a few days of this Emmeline fell ill and was removed to the prison hospital. Neither she nor the others completed their sentence, for they were all released unexpectedly a few days before the sentence ended.

In the meantime yet another women's suffrage measure had been defeated in the House of Commons. The W.S.P.U. had organized a monster protest meeting at Albert Hall in London. On the platform Emmeline's usual place as chairman was empty save for a placard reading, "Mrs. Pankhurst's chair." No one knew she had been released from Holloway. When, looking pale and worn, she stepped onto the platform, thousands of women rose to their feet, wildly cheering and applauding.

But troubles were piling up against them. In the spring of 1908 Sir Henry Campbell-Bannerman resigned the office of Prime Minister owing to ill health, his place was taken by Mr. Asquith. Although Sir Henry had done nothing to help the cause, he was personally sympathetic toward it. Mr. Asquith, however, was not sympathetic, and he detested the way the suffragettes were behaving—the marches, the noisy scuffles with the police, the arrests and imprisonments.

To the W.S.P.U. Mr. Asquith was now *the* enemy. When he first took office he hinted that the suffrage question might be dealt with by a free vote of the House—with every member voting as he chose and not according to a party line—in the lifetime of the present Parliament; yet a week or so later, when challenged to make his position clear, he had spoken loftily of such a debate being held only in "a remote and speculative future." The Home Secretary, Herbert Gladstone, was more honest. He was a supporter of votes for women, although he considered that at first only a small number of women should be enfranchised. But he admitted that if a really large body of women demanded the vote their demand would have some influence on the Government.

This was a good excuse for Emmeline to prove the strength of her following. A monster demonstration was therefore planned to take place in Hyde Park on Midsummer Day. There were to be seven processions into the Park and twenty platforms; for weeks beforehand leaflets and posters were distributed in London and the provinces showing the routes the processions were to take.

A few days before the demonstration members of Parliament and their wives and friends were drinking tea on the

Invitation to the Hyde Park Demonstration

terrace of the House of Commons overlooking the River Thames. Suddenly they heard a powerful voice calling to them from a decorated launch on the river, "Come to the Park on Sunday. You will have police protection, and there will be no arrests, we promise you."

The voice belonged to the General. She had hired the launch for the occasion and had steamed up the river with a number of friends. A member of Parliament rushed away to telephone for police boats, but by the time they arrived on the scene the suffragette launch had steamed away.

Midsummer Day was gloriously fine. As Emmeline marched into Hyde Park at the head of the first of the seven processions she saw that crowds were pouring into the Park from all directions. She climbed on to the platform and stood looking down on the crowd with delighted surprise. She had counted on an audience of at least 250,000, but the next day *The Times* newspaper correspondent suggested that there might well have been double that number. And, wherever she looked, Emmeline saw women in light summer dresses and huge, flower-trimmed hats proudly wearing the new suffragette colors—purple, white, and green—which Emmeline Pethick-Lawrence had devised.

Speeches were made from the twenty platforms; a resolution was sent by special messenger to the Prime Minister; and the war cry, "Votes for Women," was thundered three times. Then the crowds turned and dispersed in a quiet and orderly fashion; the demonstration was over.

The Prime Minister replied to the resolution, but his reply was disappointingly vague, and added nothing at all to his last statement.

Mr. Asquith needed another reminder, thought Emmeline, and a few days later the Women's Parliament met at Caxton Hall again. A resolution was passed and, with Mrs. Pethick-Lawrence and eleven other women, Emmeline set out for Parliament, leaving a number of volunteers for prison to try and hold a public meeting in Parliament Square.

The delegation was turned back at the Stranger's Entrance to the House of Commons. Meanwhile, the police were busy breaking up the meeting. Suffragettes clung to the railings of Palace Yard and the Abbey gardens until dragged away by force. The police were rough, but the hooligans who mingled with the crowd in Parliament Square were far rougher. They were out for a fight, and the unfortunate women got the worst of it.

Watching the fight from the safety of Palace Yard were a number of Parliament members, among them David Lloyd George, the Chancellor of the Exchequer, and Herbert Gladstone, the Home Secretary.

In the midst of the confusion two of the women managed to worm their way out of the crowd and make their way by taxi to Downing Street. They threw stones at the windows of the Prime Minister's official residence, No. 10, and when several windows had been broken, the two women were arrested.

While they were waiting to be charged they sent a message to Mrs. Pankhurst. As they had acted without orders, they said, they could not expect Headquarters to support them.

But Emmeline hurried to see them, and to assure them that she quite approved of their action. Window breaking was a new weapon; it was one which was to be used frequently in the future.

The two women were sent to prison for two months. One of them was Mary Leigh, who had hung a "Votes for Women" banner over the witness box the last time she was charged. Twenty-nine other arrests were made in Parliament Square, and sentences ranged from one to three months.

The offenses which had been committed were not very serious, but Emmeline now made up her mind to get herself arrested for a really serious crime in order to draw attention to the injustice with which the women's cause was being treated. A poster was therefore printed giving notice of a public meeting to be held in Trafalgar Square. "Men and women," read the poster, "help the suffragettes to RUSH the House of Commons."

To invite the public to attack the House of Commons, the seat of government, was illegal, as Emmeline well knew. But the invitation was repeated at the meeting, at which Emmeline, Christabel, and the General spoke from the base of the Nelson Column. Warrants for their arrest were issued on the ground that they had been guilty of conduct likely to provoke a breach of the peace. The women were ordered to appear at Bow Street the same afternoon, but they did nothing of the sort. Instead, they turned up at the usual suffragette reception at Queen's

Hall, where they were greeted with extra warmth and affection. No one tried to arrest them, but a police officer brought a message to the hall that the summons had been adjourned until the next morning.

"It does not suit our convenience to obey the summons quite so early," wrote Emmeline loftily in a note to the police. "We shall be in our headquarters, No. 4 Clement's Inn, at six o'clock tomorrow evening, and will then be entirely at your disposal."

The whole of the next day was spent by Emmeline and Christabel on the roof garden of the Pethick-Lawrences' flat in Clement's Inn, sorting out papers and making preparations for a long absence. At six precisely they walked downstairs to the office. There they were joined

Christabel Pankhurst in Trafalgar Square (1908)

by the General, and by the police officers who had come to arrest them.

It was too late in the evening for the women to be charged, so they spent the night at Bow Street police station. When he heard the news one of Emmeline's sympathizers—a Liberal member of Parliament—ordered a magnificent dinner to be sent to Bow Street from the

Arrest of Mrs. Pankhurst, Christabel Pankhurst, and Mrs. Drummond (left)—October 13, 1908.

Savoy Hotel, and the women were allowed to eat it in the matron's office.

Next morning their case came up and was adjourned for a week, the accused being released on bail. During that week a delegation to Parliament from the Women's Parliament had another skirmish with the police in Parliament Square, and twenty-four women and ten men were arrested and sent to prison. For the second time the fight was watched by the Chancellor of the Exchequer, who had with him his small daughter Megan.

The leaders were tried in October, accused of inciting their followers to break the peace by rushing the House of Commons. The court was crammed with spectators, and there were journalists from all the leading newspapers in the press seats.

Christabel conducted the defense. She had earned a law degree and, although she had never appeared at the Bar, she knew the procedure and had managed to subpoena the Home Secretary and the Chancellor of the Exchequer, who had watched the disturbance, to give evidence. Christabel had plenty of brilliance and dash and conducted the case with assurance. Before long she had made both the Home Secretary and the Chancellor look uncomfortable, particularly the Chancellor.

A good deal depended on the exact meaning of the word "rush." The prosecution argued that by inviting people to rush the House of Commons the suffragette leaders were inciting them to violence. With this argument Lloyd George agreed.

"I find that in *Chambers' English Dictionary* one of the

meanings of the word is 'an eager demand,' " said Christabel mildly. "Now, if you were asked to help the suffragettes to make an eager demand to the House of Commons that they should give votes to women, would you feel that we were calling upon you to do an illegal act?"

"That is not for me to say," replied Lloyd George.

"Did I or Mrs. Pankhurst threaten violence to any member of the Government?" Christabel demanded. "Did we invite the audience to attack you in any way?"

The Chancellor had to admit that they had not.

Under further questioning he also had to admit that he had his six-year-old daughter with him during the so-called "rush" from Caxton Hall to Parliament which had followed the Trafalgar Square meeting.

"You thought it was quite safe for a child of that age to be among the crowd?"

"I was not among the crowd," snapped the Chancellor. "I only brought her from Downing Street to the House."

But Christabel had made her point. If he had really feared that the suffragettes intended to attack the House of Commons he would have kept his little daughter at home. She also caught him on another point. He himself on another occasion had used far more violent words than the suffragettes; for when he addressed a meeting in his contituency, he had advised his supporters that the women should be ruthlessly flung out of the hall.

In spite of Christabel's sparkling defense there was really no question that the defendants would be found guilty. Emmeline had also questioned some of the witnesses and, when Christabel had delivered her speech for the defense, her mother made her own speech. Her manner was quiet and calm, her voice clear and even, though with a mournful undertone. She began by protesting against the Government's malice in persecuting the suffragettes. Then she spoke of her earlier life.

"I married a man whose wife I was," she said, addressing the magistrate, "but I was also his comrade in all his public life. He was, as you know, sir, a distinguished member of your own profession, but he felt it his duty, in addition, to do public work, to interest himself in the welfare of his fellow countrymen."

She also spoke of her own public work, as Poor Law Guardian, as a member of a school board, and Registrar of Births and Deaths; she described some of the injustices which women had to bear in a country in which they had no political freedom. "Great suffering is endured by women because of the state of the law. . . . Many women have thought as I have and for many, many years have tried to alter the law. We have presented petitions and we have held meetings greater than men have ever held for any reform. We have faced hostile mobs at street corners because we were told we could not have our political rights unless we converted the whole of the country to our side. We have been misrepresented and we have been ridiculed; contempt has been poured upon us. We have faced the violence of ignorant mobs, unprotected by the safeguards provided for Cabinet Ministers."

The magistrate, a dignified and handsome man, who had been frowning and angry while Christabel examined the witnesses, listened quietly, his face half hidden by his hand.

"I am here now, sir," continued Emmeline, her voice gaining strength, "to take upon myself the full responsibility for this agitation. I want you to realize that if you decide to bind us over we shall not sign any undertaking. So if you decide against us, to prison we must go, because we feel that if we consented to be bound over we should be going back to the hopeless condition this movement was in three years ago. We are driven to this; we are determined to go on with the agitation; we are in honor bound to do so until we win. We believe that if we get the vote it will mean changed conditions for our less fortunate sisters." She drew herself up defiantly. "If you had power to send us to prison, not for six months, but for six years, or for the whole of our lives, the Government must not think they could stop this agitation; it would go on. We are here, not because we are lawbreakers; we are here in our efforts to become lawmakers."

Emmeline's voice died away. For a moment the magistrate put his hand over his eyes, while several of the police, who had arrested suffragettes before and would do so again, had tears on their faces.

Nevertheless, as the defendants refused to be bound over to keep the peace, Emmeline and the General were sentenced to three months' imprisonment and Christabel to ten weeks'.

CHAPTER 9

Prison Mutiny

THE gates of Holloway prison had scarcely been locked behind her before Emmeline began to protest. The prisoners had been sentenced to imprisonment in the second division, which meant that they would be given the medium severe treatment meted out to criminals. Political prisoners were always put in the first division and given more lenient treatment. Suffragettes were not ordinary criminals but political offenders, declared Emmeline, and she demanded the right of political offenders to speak to their fellow prisoners, wear their own clothes, and receive visitors, letters, and books.

Her demands were sent to the Home Secretary, who turned them down. This made no difference to Emmeline. On the following Sunday as the prisoners silently left chapel she called after her daughter who was going back to her cell, "Christabel, stand still till I come to you."

Christabel did as she was told. Her mother came running to her, took her arm, and started to talk in a low voice.

The woman guard on duty raced toward them. "I shall listen to everything you say," she said.

"You are welcome to do that," replied Emmeline coldly, "but I shall insist on my right to speak to my daughter."

The woman blew her whistle for reinforcements. When they arrived mother and daughter were rushed back to their cells, while the other suffragettes, who had been sentenced before them, were hustled across the prison yard. As a punishment, Emmeline was told that she would be deprived of exercise and chapel until she promised not to speak again.

News of the "mutiny" reached the outside world through a prisoner whose sentence had expired. Questions were asked in the House of Commons about the treatment the suffragettes were having and, as a result, Emmeline and Christabel were given permission to meet for an hour a day and to see the newspapers if they wished.

When the three leaders were released—and neither Emmeline, Christabel, nor the General served her full term—they found a carriage drawn by white horses awaiting them. A large and sympathetic crowd had gathered to give them a rousing welcome. Led by girls dressed in the suffragette colors of purple, white, and green, they were escorted at the head of a procession to a welcome-home breakfast.

While they were in prison there had been demonstrations in the House of Commons. Men had called down protests from the Strangers' Gallery, and in the Ladies' Gallery three members of Mrs. Despard's Women's Freedom League had chained themselves so securely to the grill that they could not be released. Officials of the

House put their hands over the women's mouths to stifle their cries of "Votes for Women!" The police were called, and they had to remove the grill and the women before they could set the women free. Afterward, of course, the offenders were all sent to Holloway prison.

More and more women were now becoming militant suffragettes and were being sent to prison. As a protest against the rough treatment given by the police to delegations from the Women's Parliament, windows in a number of Government offices were broken. Cabinet Ministers were heckled so fiercely whenever they opened their

A triumphant exit from the prison gates (1908)

mouths to speak in public that their meetings were now declared closed to women. But the suffragettes were an agile band. On a number of occasions they climbed onto the roof of a hall where a meeting was being held and let themselves down through a skylight.

Once when the Prime Minister went to speak in Birmingham, two suffragettes—Mary Leigh, who had already been in prison twice, and a tall, pretty girl named Charlotte Marsh—found to their annoyance that every possible way into the hall had been barred. They

Arrest of a suffragette (1909)

therefore climbed onto a neighboring roof, each armed with an ax, and proceeded to hack off slates and fling them on the roof of the hall with such force that the people inside the hall could not hear the speeches. A fire engine was summoned and hoses played on the women until they were drenched. They refused to move, and continued to throw slates on the roof and into the street until the police clambered up to the roof, dragged them down, and marched them, still dripping with water, to the nearest police station.

By this time many of the suffragettes sent to prison were not only protesting their right to be treated as political offenders but were also refusing to eat. This hunger-striking, as it was called, was a powerful weapon. The prison authorities could not afford to let the women die of starvation and so had to release them as soon as their health showed signs of failing. But by the time Mary Leigh and Charlotte Marsh were arrested in Birmingham the authorities had devised a countermeasure; and Emmeline, who thoroughly approved of hunger-striking, was horrified when she learned that the prisoners were being forcibly fed. A length of rubber tubing was thrust through their mouths, or up their nostrils, and into their throat, and through it liquid food such as milk or beef-tea was poured.

Forcible feeding is always a disgusting process, but when the patient struggles, it can also be extremely painful and may cause injuries. When she was released Mary Leigh brought an action against the Home Secretary in which she claimed that forcible feeding was illegal. She lost, and the horrible business continued.

About the same time a thin young woman with green eyes and red hair was arrested in Manchester for interrupting a meeting. Her name was Emily Wilding-Davison, and she was a graduate of Oxford University. After being forcibly fed once Emily Wilding-Davison was so sickened at the thought of enduring the torment again that she managed to barricade herself into her cell. As the door could not be opened a hosepipe was turned on her through the tiny window in the door and, with the icy-cold water rising about her, she was obliged to give in.

Emily Wilding-Davison was one of a large number of intellectual or artistic women who had become suffragettes. There were writers, musicians, painters, and dancers among them, as well as the wives and daughters of politicians and other distinguished families. Sometimes the families approved, but more often than not they were furious that their womenfolk should make themselves so conspicuous. One of the best known was Lady Constance Lytton, the delicate, forty-year-old daughter of the second Earl of Lytton. Lady Constance, who was tall and slim with a long, gentle face, was very shy, but she was determined to overcome her timidity and her hatred of publicity by taking part in a disturbance which would send her to prison. She therefore went to Newcastle, and while several other suffragettes bombarded the windows of the post office and the Liberal Club with stones, she threw a brick at the car which was taking a member of the Government to a meeting.

Emily Wilding-Davison

All the offenders were arrested. Lady Constance was fined £4. She refused to pay and was sent to prison for a month. In prison she went on a hunger strike, as did the others. She was not forcibly fed, but after three days of hunger-striking, she and another prisoner whose husband was a public figure were released.

Before being forcibly fed prisoners were examined by a doctor, but the examination was very brief and not at all thorough. The doctor who had examined Lady Constance had said that she had a diseased heart and that forcible feeding would endanger her health. She was well aware that her heart was weak, but she had a shrewd idea that if she had not been Lady Constance Lytton the doctor would have found her heart quite strong enough. What could she do to force the authorities to treat her as they treated her friends?

On a cold January day in the year 1910 a tall, shabbily dressed woman took the train from London to Liverpool. On her short, roughly cut hair she wore a battered hat; there were ugly, steel-rimmed spectacles on her nose, and on the lapel of her long, dark coat she wore three cheap-looking brooches. Outside Walton Jail the woman climbed onto a soapbox and began to speak, while a small crowd of spectators gathered around her.

"Women are being forcibly fed inside this very prison," cried the woman. "If there are no men in Liverpool to stand up for the prisoners, who are asking no more than the vote, let the women do their part. I call upon you all to follow me to the Governor's house."

The woman climbed down from her soapbox and

strode off, the crowd at her heels. She picked up some stones and began to hurl them over the hedge which enclosed the garden of the prison Governor's house; the police promptly arrested her.

At the police station she gave her name as Jane Warton and said she was a seamstress by trade. When a woman guard examined the brooches pinned to the woman's coat, she found that each carried a portrait—one of Mrs. Pankhurst, one of Christabel, and the third of Mrs. Pethick-Lawrence.

Jane Warton was sentenced to fourteen days' hard labor.

"I shall refuse to eat," she said.

For three days they let her alone and she ate nothing. Then she was forcibly fed, after the doctor had examined her briefly and declared her to be perfectly fit.

All the suffragettes suffered when they were forcibly fed, but Jane Warton was so terribly sick and ill that the doctor whose job it was to push the rubber tubing down her throat begged her to give up her hunger strike.

She refused, and the hideous business of forcible feeding went on.

Within a few days, however, she was suddenly released, without an explanation. The truth was that the Governor had been shown a newspaper clipping which said that the prisoner was not plain Jane Warton but Lady Constance Lytton, as, of course, she was.

After her release Lady Constance wrote to the Home Secretary complaining that the prison authorities had one rule for the working classes, another for the rich. When she was sent to prison under her own name she was told that she had a serious heart condition and could not stand forcible feeding. As Jane Warton her heart had been pronounced perfectly sound, and there was no question of her not being forcibly fed.

Lady Constance was an extremely brave woman. She had known all along that her heart might not stand the strain, and shortly after her release she was taken gravely ill. She recovered sufficiently to go on working for the cause, but the illness, after which she never really regained her strength, was certainly caused in part by her experiences in prison.

Lady Constance Lytton

It was through Lady Constance that a brilliant woman musician and composer came into the movement. Her name was Ethel Smyth; she was to become famous as the composer of a great deal of music, including two operas, *The Wreckers* and *The Boatswain's Mate.* At this time she had just been awarded an honorary degree as Doctor of Music by the University of Durham. Her friend, Lady Constance Lytton, wrote to congratulate her, and also to take the opportunity to ask her for her views on the suffrage question, especially on the question of militant tactics, such as window breaking.

Ethel Smyth, a most forceful and amusing woman, had to confess that she had no views on the suffrage question at all. She was so busy with her work, which often kept her out of England, that she had no time to think of anything else.

She was preparing to write and tell Lady Constance this when she met Emmeline Pankhurst at a reception. Emmeline, who had heard that the musician did not belong to any suffrage society, greeted her rather coldly when they were introduced. But they had only been talking for a few minutes when Ethel Smyth fell under the spell which made so many women eager to follow where Emmeline led.

After their first meeting a close friendship sprang up between the two women, and Ethel Smyth promised to give the next two years of her life to the cause. During these years she would forget all about her music and work with the militants under Emmeline's leadership. When the two years were over, however, she must be free to go back to her own work.

At the beginning of the hunger-strike campaign Emmeline had decided to go on a short lecture tour of America. She had two reasons for going. The first was to gain sympathy and funds for the cause; the second was to earn some money to pay for medical care for her son.

Harry Pankhurst had always been delicate. He was no longer apprenticed to the Glasgow builder, who had failed in business, but was now working on an experimental farm in Essex. The work was heavy and the boy had become ill. Emmeline was on the point of starting for America when she learned that he had been stricken with a second illness, infantile paralysis, and was paralyzed from the waist down.

Sick at heart, Emmeline was torn between going and staying. In the end she decided to go, leaving Harry in a nursing home run by two suffragette nurses, Miss Townend and Miss Pine, and cared for by his Aunt Mary and his sisters.

In spite of her anxiety about Harry, Emmeline's American tour was an immense success. First came a whirl of receptions and press interviews. When the time came for her first lecture—in New York's Carnegie Hall—she had no idea at all how her speech would be received.

The hall was filled to overflowing with people anxious to see this dangerous, warlike figure in the flesh. What they saw was a slight, middle-aged woman, with a face which was still beautiful and a quiet, controlled manner.

Emmeline looked gravely about the hall. "I am what you call a hooligan," she said.

The contrast between the gentle-looking woman on the platform and the words she had spoken was so great that the whole audience broke into shouts of friendly laughter.

After this Emmeline knew that she had the audience with her. She went on to tell them how passionately she and her friends in England believed in their cause, and of the methods they were using in their fight for the vote. She described the window breaking, the heckling of Cabinet Ministers, the arrests, imprisonments, and hunger strikes. Her audience applauded and cheered her.

Everywhere she went Emmeline received a tremendous welcome. In Boston a large gray car decorated with the suffragette colors took her to the meeting place. In Baltimore her stewards were professors and students from Johns Hopkins University. And on a visit to Canada which followed she was given an official welcome by the Mayor of Toronto.

She left America toward the end of 1909, promising to return as soon as her work allowed. The lecture tour had been even more successful than she had hoped, and she traveled home in a glow of happiness.

Her homecoming was a sad one. Harry was now desperately ill, and he could not recover. For the last weeks of his life she never left his side. When he died she looked suddenly old, broken, and bowed.

CHAPTER 10

Black Friday

HOWEVER deep her sorrow at Harry's death, Emmeline put it aside and plunged once more into work for the movement.

The year 1910 was called by the suffragettes the year of truce. A general election held in January brought the Liberals back to power with a greatly reduced majority. On the eve of the election Mr. Asquith had said that if a reform bill were to be introduced with an amendment on women's suffrage, the amendment would be open to a free vote in the House of Commons.

After the election a committee was set up composed of Parliament members belonging to the three political parties. The Chairman was Lord Lytton, the brother of Lady Constance. The work of the committee was to examine the question of women's suffrage and to see if the vote could be given to some—if not all—women. The committee was known as the Conciliation Committee, and all through the spring and early summer it was busy working out the terms of a conciliation bill.

When Emmeline heard about this she was delighted. "It's beginning to look as though the Government will give way," she said, "and so we must do nothing to hamper the committee's work. There will be no window breaking or any other illegal acts until we know exactly how we stand."

By June the committee was ready with a conciliation bill which aimed at giving the vote to women householders and the occupiers of business premises on which not less than £10 a year was paid in taxes.

The previous month King Edward VII had died and had been succeeded by his son King George V. To herald the new reign, and also the introduction of the conciliation bill in the House of Commons, the W.S.P.U. decided to hold a vast procession through the streets of London. All the suffrage societies took part, and there were men's societies working for women's suffrage as well as women's societies. The procession was so long that Emmeline reckoned that it took an hour and a half to pass any given point. At the head marched Mary Leigh, the slight, determined woman who had been the first to suffer forcible feeding. Next came Mrs. Pankhurst and Christabel with Mrs. Pethick-Lawrence marching between them. Emmeline's dark dress was covered by a white cloak and Mrs. Pethick-Lawrence wore a white suit. The elder women wore large flowered hats, and Christabel, who was bareheaded, wore her academic robes over a white blouse and skirt.

Immediately behind the leaders came more than six hundred white-clad women. Each one of them—the leaders included—carried a tall silver-colored staff tipped with a broad arrow, to signify that she had been in prison. All along the route the ex-prisoners were given especially warm cheers.

The procession ended at Albert Hall, where Lord Lytton presided over a great demonstration.

"It now remains with the Government to help the passage of the concilation bill into law," said Lord Lytton. "We have every reason to be confident."

Then the treasurer of the W.S.P.U., Mrs. Pethick-Lawrence, told the meeting that £5,000 had just been collected for the campaign fund. Christabel Pankhurst and Annie Kenney followed with speeches on the work which had already been done.

Finally, Emmeline rose to a terrific burst of cheering to speak a single sentence. "We have only one word in our thoughts today," she said, "and that word is victory."

Their high hopes were soon to be dashed. Many Parliament members supported the conciliation bill in the House of Commons, and for the first time the women's suffrage question was argued with seriousness instead of being greeted with laughter and jeers. All the same, the bill was shelved. It was not dropped, but it was put aside indefinitely, and the right to vote seemed no nearer than it ever had been.

A delegation of Liberal women from his own constituency then called on the Prime Minister to ask if the bill could not be advanced if not in 1910, then in the following year. Mr. Asquith's reply infuriated the suffragettes. "Wait and see," was all he said.

Until this point Emmeline had held her hand. But, now that it was becoming likely that the conciliation bill would be shelved for good, she resolved to start the militant fight again. A meeting was called at Albert Hall at which she broke the news to her followers.

"If the bill, in spite of our efforts, is killed by the Government, then there is an end of the truce," she solemnly declared. "If we are met by the statement that there is no power to secure on the floor of the House of Commons time for our measure, then our next step is to say, 'We take it out of your hands, since you fail to help us, and we resume the direction of the campaign ourselves.' But first, one more delegation must go to the Prime Minister. I will lead it myself, and if no one cares to follow me, I will go alone."

From all parts of the hall came cries of support. "I will go with you, Mrs. Pankhurst." "And I!" "And I!"

In the end, 450 women were chosen to march to Parliament on a given date—Friday, November 18. Some were to start from Caxton Hall, others from the W.S.P.U. headquarters, and they were ordered to go in small numbers, with intervals between, and to march in single file, according to the law.

The leaders were Emmeline herself and a very distinguished suffragist. She was the pioneer woman doctor, seventy-four-year-old Elizabeth Garrett Anderson, a sister of the suffragist leader, Mrs. Fawcett. Mrs. Garrett Anderson wore a black cloak edged with fur and a fur bonnet tied under her chin with white strings. Emmeline wore a warm coat over her long black dress, and her black hat was secured by a veil.

The dignified presence of Mrs. Garrett Anderson so

impressed the police that they made a way through the waiting crowd for the leading group of women and escorted them to the House of Commons.

A party of sympathetic Parliament members received them, but, when they asked to be taken to the Prime Minister, they were told that he would not see them. They

Dr. Elizabeth Garrett Anderson and Mrs. Pankhurst

therefore gathered in a group on the steps of the St. Stephen's entrance while their followers advanced into Parliament Square.

In a sense they were prisoners, for the way back was blocked, and they had to stand and watch the most brutal fight that had yet taken place. They had known that many women would be arrested that day. But now the police seemed to be deliberately obstructing the suffragettes and doing them as much injury as possible before actually arresting them. Emmeline saw women tripped up, knocked down, punched in the face and body, and kicked as they lay on the ground. And, as always, there were plenty of hooligans in the crowd who hit and kicked far more savagely than the police.

The horrible struggle went on all through the afternoon; it ended finally with 117 arrests—115 women and two men. Next morning all the offenders were released without being charged. Perhaps the authorities felt that the police had exceeded their duties. More likely, thought Emmeline grimly, it was because there was another general election in the offing and the Government would not risk losing the votes of men who might think that the women had been badly treated.

Friday, November 18, was known ever afterward as "Black Friday." It was a landmark in the fight for the vote because it put an end to the truce which Emmeline had called so hopefully earlier in the year.

The Women's Parliament met the following day. A vague statement was read to the audience about the intentions of the Liberal Party if it were to be reelected to power at the forthcoming general election.

"This is not good enough," cried Emmeline. "I'm going to Downing Street. Come along, all of you."

The entire meeting streamed behind her out into the street. The police, taken by surprise, gave way and the women surged toward Downing Street. Some actually reached No. 10 before they were caught and seized. Emmeline and more than a hundred were arrested. But, as on Black Friday, no charges were made against them and they were released. Many of the women then broke windows in order to get themselves rearrested, and this time they were convicted and sent to prison.

One of the window breakers was Emmeline's younger sister, Mary Clarke. Mary had followed Emmeline's lead ever since that far-off day in their childhood when they had "demonstrated" outside the polling booth and been hustled home in disgrace. She had been a second mother to Emmeline's children and was dearly loved by the whole family. But despite her gentleness Mary Clarke was a woman of great courage. Although she was delicate and knew she could not stand the hardships of prison life for long, she did not hesitate to break the law and get herself convicted.

Two days before Christmas Mary was released from prison to join Emmeline at the home of one of their brothers. During Christmas Day dinner she quietly left the table saying that she was rather tired and would lie down for a little while. When Emmeline followed a few minutes later she found her loyal, devoted sister unconscious and dying.

It was not quite a year since Harry's death, and Emmeline was heartbroken. Yet immediately after the funeral, white-faced and tight-lipped, she went back to work.

At the general election the Liberals were again returned to power, and Mr. Asquith said that he hoped that time would be found to consider an amendment on women's suffrage to the conciliation bill some time in 1911 or 1912. Cheered by this news, Emmeline went on a second lecture tour of Canada and the United States. Like the first tour, it was an immense success. Everywhere she went Emmeline found herself hailed as a great leader.

She was still in America when she learned that the concilation bill had finally been killed. It had not actually been dropped, but Mr. Asquith had announced that his Government intended to bring in a franchise bill of its own. This bill would extend the vote to all men, but nothing at all was said about women. Everyone knew that when the Government bill was introduced the conciliation bill had absolutely no chance of survival.

"Protest imperative!" cabled Emmeline from America.

Her followers went into action at once. A raiding party led by Mrs. Pethick-Lawrence, with hammers and stones hidden in their handbags and muffs, smashed windows in a number of Government offices and the houses of members of the Government. Two hundred and twenty-three women were arrested, and 150 of them sent to prison for terms ranging from five days to a month.

Other window-smashing raids followed. It was not

easy to find enough stones of the right kind in the streets of London. After dark respectable-looking cars were driven out of London into flinty country lanes, to return later loaded with ammunition.

Then a new weapon was discovered. Emily Wilding-Davison, who had once barricaded herself in her cell to avoid being forcibly fed, was caught in Parliament Square pushing a piece of burning linen through a post office box. Other suffragettes followed her example and began to set fire to Government property.

Private property was also suffering by this time, and shop windows all over the West End of London were being broken. Raiding parties made up of fashionably dressed women were carefully drilled. While one innocent-looking party smashed windows and got itself arrested, another party went into action nearby. A great deal of damage was done in this way, and a large number of arrests were made.

When Emmeline returned from America to take charge of the campaign she decided that she needed some stone-throwing practice. She therefore went down to Woking in Surrey to stay with her musician friend, Ethel Smyth, who was extremely athletic and a very good shot.

Ethel Smyth took Emmeline at dusk to a secluded part of Hook Heath and dumped a collection of stones near a large fir tree.

"Now, Em, throw," she said, "and see how often you can hit that tree."

Emmeline did as she was told. The first stone flew backward out of her hand, almost hitting Ethel's shaggy sheep dog, lying at his mistress's feet.

"You'd better stand a bit nearer. Try it from three yards' distance."

Emmeline moved nearer the target. She threw a number of stones, which all fell very wide of the mark.

Ethel Smyth tried hard not to laugh, for with each failure her friend's face became more and more ferocious.

It was obvious that Emmeline would have the greatest difficulty in breaking a window. In the end, however, a stone hit the tree with a dull thud. At once the scowl on Emmeline's face was replaced by a beaming smile. She turned to her friend for congratulation, only to find her doubled up on the ground, quite helpless with laughter.

A few days later the two friends went by taxi to Downing Street, where both were arrested for breaking windows. But, while the musician broke her window with the first stone, she noticed that Emmeline's stones had all gone wide of the mark.

On this occasion more than two hundred women were arrested for window breaking in different parts of London. While their trials were being held the police raided the W.S.P.U. headquarters in Clement's Inn and arrested Mr. and Mrs. Pethick-Lawrence. Christabel would also have been arrested, had she been there. But she was out at the time, and when she heard of the raid, she escaped from the country and went to Paris. There she took a flat under an assumed name. Since the other leaders had now been arrested, she made up her mind to run the W.S.P.U. from abroad and to edit its paper, *Votes for Women,* herself.

Emmeline and the Pethick-Lawrences appeared at the Bow Street police court, and were committed for trial at the Old Bailey on a charge of "conspiring to incite certain persons to commit malicious damage to property." Meanwhile, Emmeline, with Ethel Smyth, had been sentenced to two months' imprisonment for breaking windows.

There were now so many suffragettes in Holloway prison that the whole of one wing was given over to them. For the time being they were allowed to do much as they pleased. One of them, a ballet dancer, sent home for her ballet skirts and danced to amuse the company. The prisoners came from all walks of life. There were writers, artists, and musicians among them, as well as nurses, typists, shopgirls, and women of the poorer classes, many of whom had lost their jobs by being sent to prison. Yet not one of them counted the cost or was bitter at losing her job. They were united in devotion to their leader and in the belief that the vote was the most important thing in life and that going to prison was the only way to get it. The knowledge that their adored Mrs. Pankhurst was among them made prison life seem almost enjoyable.

Somehow or other the younger and more athletic prisoners contrived to hang the prison yard with banners of purple, white, and green. Others formed themselves into a choir under Ethel Smyth's direction. She had written the music for the suffrage song, and they were fond of singing it. One day a party of them were plodding around the yard during their exercise hour when they looked up to see Ethel Smyth at the high barred window of her cell. Immediately they stopped, and started to sing,

Shout, shout—up with your song,
Cry with the wind, for the dawn is breaking.
March, march, swing you along.
Wide blows our banner and hope is waking.
Song with its story, dreams with their glory,
Lo! they call and glad is their word;
Hark, hark, how it swells,
Thunder of freedom, the voice of the Lord.

Smiling down at the suffragettes as they sang stood the composer, beating time to the music with her toothbrush.

It was not all fun and singing in Holloway. The suffragettes had orders to make themselves troublesome. They demanded permission to speak to Mrs. Pankhurst. This was refused, whereupon the prisoners protested noisily. The women guards thrust them by force into their cells, where they retaliated by smashing windows and any other breakable objects they could find. Many went on hunger strikes and endured the horrors of forcible feeding.

The chilly, damp cell in which Emmeline was confined for the greater part of every day gave her a bad cold which led to bronchitis. She was still weak when her trial for conspiracy came on at Old Bailey in May, 1912. It was not difficult for the prosecution to prove that the two Emmelines—Pankhurst and Pethick-Lawrence—had incited their followers to damage Government and private property. Reports of their speeches proved this, and so did letters and papers written in code which the police had seized when they raided the W.S.P.U. headquarters.

Mr. Pethick-Lawrence, who had given so much time and money to the movement, conducted his own defense. "I am not part of this organization, being a man," he said, "but I intended and I still intend to stand by the women who are fighting in this agitation and using methods which I know have succeeded in history. The breaking of windows is repugnant to me, but the women who have taken this course had been driven . . . to do what they did, and I for one am not going to condemn their action. Long before any stone throwing occurred, women were arrested while going on a peaceful march to the House of Commons."

It was a brave speech by a brave man. Emmeline Pankhurst followed, to repeat the history of the suffragette movement and tell the dreadful story of Black Friday. "The police," she said, "showed a kind of ferocity in dealing with us which compelled us to take this other step. We are not the kind of people who like to brag a lot; we are not the kind of people who would like to bring ourselves into this position unless we were convinced that it were the only way." She did not attempt to deny the charge of conspiracy. "We are content to abide by the verdict of posterity," was all she said.

The judge's summary was very much against the three prisoners. But the jury, though finding them guilty, asked for a lenient sentence, realizing that, even though it was wrong for the leaders to incite their followers to damage property, they had been acting from the highest motives.

The judge sentenced the prisoners to nine months' imprisonment in the second division, Mr. Pethick-Lawrence in Pentonville, his wife and her friend in Holloway. They petitioned, as political prisoners and not ordinary criminals, to be given first-division privileges. Their petition was granted, but when they realized that all the other suffragettes then in prison were not to be given the same privileges, they went on a hunger strike.

At the time there were eighty suffragettes in prison—in Holloway, Brixton, and Aylesbury. When they learned that their leader had gone on a hunger strike as a protest against their treatment, most of them started a hunger strike of their own.

In the House of Commons questions were asked, especially about the treatment of the leaders. A heated argument broke out and tempers were lost.

"Be they leaders or rank and file," declared the Home Secretary in reply, "forcible feeding will be adopted if they do not take their food."

His reply caused a fresh explosion of anger.

"Will the Right Honourable Member arrange for a model of forcible feeding to be shown in the Chamber of Horrors at Madame Tussaud's waxworks exhibition?" demanded one member ironically.

Then a Labor member, shaking with rage, left his seat on the opposition benches, strode across the chamber, and shook his fist in the Prime Minister's face. "You will go down to history as the man who tortured innocent women," he cried passionately. "You ought to be driven from public life."

Until now the prison authorities had never tried forcible feeding on Emmeline, but she knew only too well what the ordeal meant to others. She had been told how every day the doctor and women guards would go from cell to cell, and how the cries, the sounds of struggle, and sickness which came from neighboring cells were almost as hard to bear as the ordeal itself.

She had been on a hunger strike for several days before any attempt was made to feed her. But one afternoon as she sat in her cell she realized, from the sounds coming from the adjoining cell, that her friend Emmeline Pethick-Lawrence was being forcibly fed. The sounds seemed to go on for hours. Mrs. Pethick-Lawrence was a strong woman, and it took several guards to overpower her.

Presently the sounds in the next cell ceased, and Emmeline heard the key turned in the door of her own cell. The door opened, and on the threshold stood the doctor and guards with the liquid food and the feeding tube.

Quick as a flash their prisoner seized the heavy earthenware water jug from the shelf and held it ready to throw.

"Mrs. Pankhurst," began the doctor, "I have orders . . ." His voice died away before the look of murderous rage on Emmeline's face.

"If any of you dare to take a step inside this cell, I shall defend myself," cried Emmeline.

The doctor took a step backward. "All right," he muttered, "tomorrow will do just as well."

The door clanged behind the prison party, and Emmeline sank down on to her wooden stool, covering her face with her hands. Tomorrow would come again, and she could not go on defending herself forever. Besides, she was already weak from five days' fasting.

But tomorrow never came for either of the Emmelines. Next day they were both released without any further attempt to feed them. In Pentonville, Mr. Pethick-Lawrence was forcibly fed for five days before his health gave way and he, too, was set free.

CHAPTER 11

Disguises and Tricks

AND so the fight went on. It never occurred to Emmeline to call a halt to the campaign of violence or to refrain from violence herself. Since she knew that sooner or later her actions would send her to prison again—and she was constantly watched by detectives—the wisest thing seemed to be to leave the running of the movement to Christabel, safe in Paris. This had been arranged even before her trial.

Since her mother and the Pethick-Lawrences were in prison Christabel had ordered Annie Kenney to take charge of the London headquarters in Emmeline's absence. Annie Kenney's instructions were brought by a trusted friend, who also carried a letter of encouragement from Christabel.

"Come quickly," Christabel wrote. "Disguise yourself, and watch closely for Scotland Yard men. Press on, and give all our loyal ones my love and my faith that each one will obey orders that will be sent through you by me, and by unity we shall win through."

Naturally the police wanted to get hold of Christabel, and they suspected that Annie might lead them to her. A few days later a middle-aged lady dressed all in black with a black veil over her face boarded the Channel steamer. It was Annie Kenney, skillfully disguised, on the first of several visits she managed to pay to her absent chief.

When she had recovered from her imprisonment Emmeline also decided to try to slip away to see Christabel in Paris and make plans for the future. She borrowed a fast car and a suffragette driver who admitted that she was very hazy about the way to the coast. They waited till dark, evaded the police, and the driver found her way to Surrey where, at an agreed point, she stopped to pick up Ethel Smyth.

Emmeline drew back in surprise when, in place of her severely dressed friend, a very smartly dressed woman with a veil and eyeglasses got in beside her.

"You'd never have recognized me, would you, Em?" demanded Ethel with a chuckle. She took off her glasses and removed her elegant hat, so that Emmeline could see she was wearing a black wig.

"I should certainly not have recognized you," Emmeline admitted. "How on earth did you get hold of these clothes?"

Ethel Smyth gave another chuckle. "I have a rich cousin," she said. "She's a terrible antisuffragette and thoroughly disapproves of me because I've been in prison. She thinks I ought to stick to my music, of course, and any other artistic jobs. So the other day, when I knew she was going to be out of London, I told her I needed some things for private theatricals, and she said I could borrow anything I wanted. Of course, Em, as a friend of yours, I'm usually shadowed by detectives. They saw me go into my cousin's house but they never saw me come out again because they didn't know, what I knew, that the house has an exit at the back as well as the front. All I had to do was to dress as you see me now, slip out of the back entrance, and get into a taxi."

Ethel Smyth had obviously thoroughly enjoyed her trick.

Her friend smiled. "I do wish, dear," she said, "you

Mrs. Pankhurst

always looked as you do now. You don't do yourself justice in those everlasting tweed skirts and plain blouses."

To this Ethel made no reply. She was hanging out of the window, giving directions to the driver, who would have been hopelessly lost in the darkness without her.

Safely arrived in Paris, Emmeline went to stay with Christabel. Mother and daughter worked out details for a new and more violent campaign. They knew that militant acts would turn some of their sympathizers into enemies, but this made no difference. The idea of using arson as a weapon had been put into their heads by Emily Wilding-Davison when she tried to set fire to the post office in Parliament Square. Fire was a terrible weapon, far more dangerous than throwing stones, yet they did not hesitate to use it. Orders were given that suffragettes should now carry gasoline cans and inflammable material, together with housebreaking tools, to empty houses, historic churches, and other buildings. But although they were instructed to do as much damage as they could, they were warned that they must be careful never to endanger human life.

As Emmeline expected, some members of the Union objected strongly to the use of such a weapon, and among them was Mrs. Pethick-Lawrence. Mr. Pethick-Lawrence also objected although, as he had pointed out at his trial, he was not a member of the W.S.P.U. The Pethick-Lawrences also thought that the time had come to stop all acts of extreme militancy, temporarily at any rate. So many influential people, they argued, had been so disgusted to hear that hunger-striking prisoners were being forcibly fed that the vote might be won without any more demonstrations of violence.

Emmeline and Christabel refused to accept this argument. Christabel came to London especially to discuss the problem, and a meeting was held at Albert Hall. When Emmeline appeared on the platform without the familiar figures of the Pethick-Lawrences the audience knew that a break between the leaders had occurred.

"Mr. and Mrs. Pethick-Lawrence," she told them, "who have given us devoted service, have left the Union, but they will continue to work outside it for the cause." She explained briefly the new setup, with Christabel leading the fight from Paris, herself in control in London when she was not in prison.

Then she turned to the future, crying in her stirring voice, "I incite this meeting to rebellion. Women, although the vote is not yet won, we who are militant are free. Remember only the freedom of the spirit and join this magnificent rebellion of the women of the twentieth century."

As always, the audience rose, cheering and applauding wildly, pledging itself anew to follow Emmeline's lead.

The movement was much the poorer for the departure of the Pethick-Lawrences. They had been magnificent fund raisers and most generous with their own money. Had they stayed, there would been some curb on acts of violence, but with their going militancy broke out more violently than before. On the orders of Emmeline and

Christabel an immense amount of damage was now being done.

"There is something which governments care for more than human life," Emmeline had told her followers at Albert Hall, "and that is the security of property, and so it is through property that we shall strike the enemy. Be militant each in your own way. Those of you who can express your militancy by facing party mobs at Cabinet Ministers' meetings—do so. Those of you who can break windows—break them. And those of you who can start fires—start them."

She had known, of course, that she was courting arrest for herself as well as her followers. "My last word to the Government," she said with intense feeling, "is . . . take me, if you dare!"

As a result of her words all sorts of new militant acts were committed. They shock us today as they shocked people then. Although a great deal of damage was done the suffragettes obeyed their instructions that human life must not be endangered. Telegraph and telephone wires were cut; paintings in picture galleries were slashed; the contents of mail boxes were burned with acids; the windows of London clubs and of Lambeth Palace, London home of the Archbishop of Canterbury, were smashed; the orchid houses at Kew Gardens were wrecked; a showcase in the jewel room at the Tower of London was broken; and the refreshment house in Regent's Park was burned to the ground. And among other outrages, a house which was being built in Surrey for the Chancellor of the

Exchequer, Mr. Lloyd George, was partly destroyed by a homemade bomb. The only clues to this outrage discovered by the police were two broken hatpins, a hairpin, some suffragette pamphlets, and a woman's boot. The culprits, Emily Wilding-Davison and some friends, were never caught.

Emmeline gloried in the deed. "We have blown up the Chancellor's house," she cried exultantly. She was arrested for inciting her followers to violence, and committed for trial.

The police-court magistrate offered to release her on bail if she would undertake not to break the law before her trial.

She gave him a withering look. "I shall give no such undertaking," she said.

The magistrate thereupon committed her to prison to await trial.

"If you send me to prison," Emmeline warned him, "I shall go on a hunger strike, and I shall be a dying woman when I come to be tried."

The magistrate had no option but to commit her to prison, and Emmeline was taken by prison truck to Holloway. She began to hunger-strike at once, but after twenty-four hours the authorities released her. Her trial, at Old Bailey, was put forward so that she would not be at liberty longer than was necessary.

Emmeline had only just been set free when her daughter Sylvia was released from prison. Sylvia, who lived and worked among the poorest people in the East End of London, had already been in prison a number of times. Her last sentence had been two months' hard labor for breaking windows.

In prison, Sylvia had thirst-struck as well as hunger-struck and, in order to get herself to the state when the authorities would be obliged to release her, she had spent the nights walking to and fro in her tiny cell. For five weeks she had endured the miseries of forcible feeding. Then, looking like a skeleton, she was released, to be nursed back to health by the two suffragette nurses, Townend and Pine.

When Emmeline saw her daughter she was shocked by her ghastly appearance. But no amount of suffering—her own, her daughter's, or anyone else's—would shake her determination that hunger-striking must continue.

Sylvia wrote an account of her imprisonment for a new paper which Christabel, in Paris, was editing—*The Suffragette*. The article caused a fresh outcry against the unbearable sufferings which were being inflicted on women. It also had another, and quite unexpected, result. It was partly due to Sylvia's article that the Home Secretary, Reginald McKenna, introduced into the House of Commons the Prisoners' Temporary Discharge for Ill-Health Bill. The bill aimed at doing away with the need for forcible feeding by letting prisoners hunger-strike until the danger point of starvation was reached. They would then be released on license—that is to say, they would be ordered to return to prison at the end of a given time.

The bill passed quickly through its various stages and

became law. The first batch of suffragettes to be arrested were allowed to hunger-strike until they had made themselves thoroughly ill. When ordered to report back to prison at the end of a week, they refused to agree to any conditions. As a result, their movements were watched by police, and they were rearrested at the earliest possible moment, in some cases before they had been nursed back to health.

The suffragettes called the new act the "Cat-and-Mouse Act." The police were now the cats, the suffragettes the mice.

The act had not yet passed into law when Emmeline came up for trial at Old Bailey. Her face was deeply lined and drawn, but her figure was as upright as ever, and her eyes burned brilliantly.

She called no evidence in her defense but addressed the court herself. "Over one thousand women have gone to prison in the course of this agitation" she said proudly, "and have come out weakened in body but not in spirit. I have come to stand my trial from the bedside of one of my daughters, who has submitted herself for more than five weeks to the horrible ordeal of feeding by force. She has lost two stones in weight. She is so weak that she cannot get out of bed." Emmeline's voice trembled as she spoke of Sylvia's pathetic condition. "This is the kind of punishment you will inflict upon me," she went on, "or any other woman who may be brought before you. I ask you if you are prepared to send an endless number of women to prison and to forcible feeding, because that is what is going to happen."

She paused for a moment, then continued defiantly. "We are, rightly or wrongly, convinced that this is the only way in which we can win power to alter what for us are intolerable conditions. Is it right that you should insist on punishing women who, because of the impossibility of getting reform of the laws that affect them very closely, are driven to take the stand they are taking? If women were free not one of us would be lawbreakers. Gentlemen of the jury, I ask you to give your verdict not solely upon my case but upon this agitation and to give a verdict of 'Not guilty.' "

In his summary the judge directed the jury to disregard Mrs. Pankhurst's arguments that women would commit no crimes if they were given the vote. The jury found her guilty, but added a strong recommendation to mercy.

"Whatever sentence you pass upon me," said Emmeline before sentence was passed, "I shall do what is humanly possible to end it. I have no sense of guilt. I feel I have done my duty."

"I find the duty of sentencing the prisoner extremely painful," said the judge. "I realize that you have not been acting from selfish motives, but your crime of inciting other women to illegal acts is both serious and wicked." In view of the jury's recommendation to mercy, he added, he would impose the lightest sentence he could—three years' penal servitude.

There was a gasp from the spectators who thronged the court. Three years' hard labor for a delicate woman seemed a savage sentence. The prisoner was taken below to cries of, "Shame!" And women filed out of court singing the suffragette song:

Shout, shout—up with your song,
Cry with the wind, for the dawn is breaking...

Emmeline heard only the first words, but they heartened her as she made ready for the journey back to prison.

CHAPTER 12

Cat and Mouse

FRESH outbreaks of violence greeted the news that Emmeline had been sentenced to three years' imprisonment. Her followers were afraid that her health would break down altogether long before the date of her release.

Inside Holloway, Emmeline went on a hunger strike. Outside the prison gates batches of suffragettes kept constant watch. Feeling ill and terribly weak, Emmeline began to think that she could not live. Perhaps, if she died, the Government would at long last relent. "If I am to die," she wrote, "good will come of my going."

But the Government had not the slightest intention of letting Emmeline die. By her death she would become a martyr and bring thousands of waverers to the cause. And so she was allowed to hunger-strike for nine days without any attempt being made to feed her by force.

Then the Governor came to her cell to tell her that she was to be set free, but only for fifteen days. At the end of that time she must return to prison and, in the meantime, she must report any change of address to the police.

Emmeline looked scornfully at the order which licensed

her release and bound her to return. She tore it up and flung the pieces on the floor.

"I have no intention of obeying this infamous law," she said furiously. "You release me knowing that I shall never voluntarily return to any of your prisons."

Two guards took Emmeline by cab to the nursing home where the suffragette nurses, Pine and Townend, were waiting to look after her. She looked most dreadfully ill —skeleton-thin, her skin parchment-yellow, her eyes sunken and burning. At first, after her long fast, she could not eat at all, but gradually her health began to improve and her appetite came back.

When the fifteen days were up two detectives and a Home Office doctor came to the nursing home to rearrest her.

"You must allow me to examine you, Mrs. Pankhurst," said the doctor. "If you are not fit to return to Holloway your license will be extended."

"I will not allow you to examine me," said Emmeline, who had sworn to make the job of the police as difficult as possible. "If you wish, you can drag me back to prison, but I shall submit to no medical examination."

The doctor realized that she was still exceedingly ill. "You are unfit to return for the present," he said. "I shall make my report to that effect."

Emmeline had no idea how long she would be left in peace, but as soon as she was well enough to travel, she slipped out of the house unnoticed and went by car to Ethel Smyth's house at Woking. Nurse Pine, a stout, strong-looking woman, went with her.

It did not take the police long to discover Emmeline's whereabouts. She had broken the terms of her license to report any change of address, and detectives were soon posted at strategic points in Ethel Smyth's half-acre garden.

The day after Emmeline's arrival was pouring with rain. Ethel Smyth, coming into Emmeline's room, looked out of the window to see two very sodden-looking detectives in the garden below. "I think I must give those poor men umbrellas," she said. "They're soaking wet already."

Emmeline tottered from her bed to the open window. "You'll do nothing of the sort," she told her friend. "Don't make things pleasant for them."

Noticing his prisoner glaring down on him from above, one of the detectives said rather pathetically, "I'm only doing my duty, Mrs. Pankhurst."

"More shame to you for doing it, then," snapped Emmeline, and slammed the window.

When the weather had improved and she was a little stronger Emmeline went to sit in the garden. But she was conscious of eyes watching her from behind trees and bushes, and knew that the police were only biding their time. As soon as she was well enough they would rearrest her.

Toward the end of May, weary of waiting, Emmeline made up her mind to try and get to London to attend a W.S.P.U. meeting. Dressed in a neat summer suit, the skirt just clear of her ankles, her hat secured by a veil, she walked calmly downstairs, accompanied by her hostess,

Nurse Pine, and Dr. Flora Murray, the woman doctor who cared for the suffragette "mice" released on license.

In reality, Emmeline was much weaker than she imagined; and her knees shook when she reached the garden gate to find two burly detectives barring the way.

"You will kindly tell me where you are going," said one of them.

Emmeline did not answer, but sank, half-fainting, into the arms of her friends.

Nurse Pine, looking like an angry bulldog, glared at the detectives as though she would like to fling them to the ground.

As soon as Emmeline showed signs of recovering the three women pushed past the detectives and helped her gently into the car which she had ordered to take her to London.

One of the detectives jumped in beside her. "Drive to Bow Street police station," he said curtly.

The driver looked embarrassed. "Mrs. Pankhurst ordered the car," he replied, "and I take my orders from her."

"Call a taxi," said the detective to his waiting companion.

Emmeline was allowed to sit in the car until the taxi arrived; then she was formally arrested, bundled into the taxi, and driven off to Bow Street.

The magistrate committed her to prison again. This time, after hunger-striking for five days, she was so pitiably feeble that she was released for a week.

It was while she was in bed in the nursing home recovering from this second bout of hunger-striking that Emmeline received a grave piece of news. Emily Wilding-Davison, always in the thick of the militant campaign, had done a brave but futile thing. On Derby Day she had gone to Epsom and had taken up her position near the rails. Just after the first horses in the Derby had passed Tattenham Corner she had run out onto the course and tried to clutch the bridle of the leader. The horse, which belonged to the King, stumbled and fell, throwing its jockey and fatally injuring the woman.

Despite every care Emily Wilding-Davison had died without regaining consciousness. The suffragettes looked on her as a martyr to their cause, but to countless other people she was a wicked woman, who might well have caused other deaths besides her own. Members of the

The death of Emily Wilding-Davison

W.S.P.U. stood guard over her coffin and marched in a long, solemn funeral procession. A carriage was ordered so that Emmeline could follow; but she could take no part, for the moment she left the nursing home she was arrested and sent back to Holloway.

This time Emmeline refused water as well as food, as Sylvia had done before her, and, like her daughter, she spent the nights tramping her cell. Within three days she had become so desperately ill that once more she was released. No further effort was ever made to feed Emmeline by force, but, as the Cat-and-Mouse Act was not working out as the authorities had hoped, and the rank and file of the movement were spending too much time out of prison, they were again being forcibly fed.

While she was free Emmeline decided to be present at a meeting which had been called at the London Pavilion to protest against the cruelty which the Act inflicted. Annie Kenney, who was also out of prison on license, decided to go too, and both of them reached the hall without being seen.

At the end of the meeting Annie calmly announced that she and Mrs. Pankhurst would leave the hall quite openly. Then she stepped quietly down from the platform. The police rushed in and, after a short but fierce struggle, she was arrested.

Thinking that Emmeline would leave by a side door, other policemen hurried to intercept her. She gave them the slip and escaped by the main entrance.

A taxi took her to the house of a friend. Within minutes the house was surrounded by a watchful body of police. As soon as Emmeline emerged they would pounce.

Not a soul went in or out of the house for two days. Then a taxi drove up and waited; several well-known suffragettes alighted and hurried inside. Presently a heavily veiled woman appeared at the door, guarded by suffragettes. The police sprang forward and, as the woman tried to climb into the taxi, her companions fought them off.

A crowd had gathered to watch the scene. "They are arresting Mrs. Pankhurst," cried someone, as the police returned to the charge.

After quite a long struggle the police tore the woman away from her friends, bundled her into the taxi, and told the driver to take them to Bow Street. On the way the woman, who had not spoken a single word, raised her veil. She was not Mrs. Pankhurst, and the angry police realized that their quarry had escaped during the struggle.

Of course Emmeline could only delay her arrest; she could not hope to avoid it. All through the summer months of 1913 she was arrested, released, and arrested again. Toward the end of August, while out on license, she actually managed to leave the country to spend two months in Paris with Christabel. The police knew very well where she was, but as she had been so desperately ill the authorities had decided to ignore the trip.

In October she made up her mind to pay another visit to the United States and sailed on a French liner. But when she reached Ellis Island in New York harbor, where immigrants are examined, she found herself detained. Scotland Yard had sent the American authorities a catalog of her crimes, and she was told that, as a person of "doubtful" character, she would be detained until the authorities in Washington had looked into her case.

"If you detain me here I shall refuse to eat," declared Emmeline.

The American authorities were not at all keen to have a hunger-striking suffragette on their hands. After two days, Emmeline was told she could enter the United States. The lecture tour which followed was even more successful than the other two, and people almost fought to get into her meetings.

With £4,500 for the cause in her pocket she embarked for England in late November on the liner *Majestic.* A wireless message from W.S.P.U. headquarters told her that she would be arrested when the liner reached Plymouth, and she knew that another period in prison awaited her.

When the liner anchored outside Plymouth, Emmeline came on deck with other passengers to find that the harbor had been cleared of all craft save for the tender which was waiting, between two large, gray battleships, to meet the ship. Then suddenly a tiny motorboat dashed past the battleships and came speeding toward the liner. Two women, drenched with spray, stood up in the boat and, as it swept past the liner, one of them called out to Emmeline, "The cats are here, Mrs. Pankhurst. They're close on you."

There was nothing Emmeline could do but wait. Presently she saw the tender approach and, within minutes, a frightened ship's messenger boy brought her a message asking her to go down to the purser's office.

"I shall do nothing of the sort," answered Emmeline, who believed that the more attention her exploits were given the better it would be for the cause. "If they want me they can come and find me."

The messenger boy scuttled away, to be replaced by a party of eight. There were five detectives from Scotland Yard, two from Plymouth, and a guard from Holloway.

"I trust you'll come quietly, Mrs. Pankhurst," said one of the men.

"I'm here to make your job as difficult as possible," replied Emmeline. She refused to move; whereupon two men picked her up and carried her, kicking and struggling, to the waiting tender.

In England, although the return to forcible feeding was lengthening the time suffragettes spent in prison, the militant campaign was still in full force. On the night of Emmeline's arrest on the *Majestic* over an acre of Plymouth timber went up in flames. Cabinet Ministers were becoming so tired of being bombarded with questions and missiles, including bags of flour, that they took to canceling meetings. The Prime Minister was actually threatened with a horse whip by a man supporter of the women's cause, and King George V was said to be very annoyed by the number of women who somehow or other contrived to thrust petitions on him.

Toward the end of the year, during one of her free periods, Emmeline escaped to Paris again. She was so weak that she had to be carried from the train to the boat, but once in Paris with Christabel, her health quickly improved. "Am wonderfully well," she wrote to Ethel Smyth, who, her two years' work for the movement being over, had returned to her beloved music. "I shall be ready for the next round on Monday," she added, "when my license is up."

Although on this occasion Emmeline had decided that it was less trouble to give herself up than to try to evade arrest, she had not given notice to the police of her intention to leave England. At Dover, therefore, two detectives pushed their way into the reserved compartment which she was sharing with her doctor and the faithful Nurse Pine. Emmeline took absolutely no notice of the detectives but stayed where she was, lying along the seat, until the train reached Victoria.

"Come along, Mrs. Pankhurst," said one of the policemen.

She closed her lips tightly and made no move.

The detectives seized her by the arms, dragged her so roughly out of the carriage that she cried out with pain, and half threw her into a waiting police car.

When she reached Holloway, Emmeline protested at this rough treatment by lying for two nights on the cold concrete floor of her cell.

On the Sunday after her arrest the congregation assembled in Westminster Abbey were disturbed by low but clear chanting. "God save Emmeline Pankhurst," sang a number of women. "Help us, with Thy love and strength, to guard her. Spare those who suffer for conscience sake." Vergers hustled the chanting women out of the Abbey, but not before an angry member of the congregation had given the woman nearest him a resounding slap on the face.

Late in December—after Emmeline had been in and out of Holloway and in yet again—her supporters made plans for a special demonstration of protest. A gala performance of an opera with Joan of Arc as its heroine was being given at Covent Garden. King George and Queen Mary were present and the opera house was gleaming with orders, jewels, and the lovely, rich colors of women's gowns.

At the close of the first act a well-dressed woman sitting in a box almost opposite the Royal Box rose to her feet and began to address the king through a megaphone. "Your Majesty," she cried, "women are fighting today as Joan of Arc fought centuries ago, and like the Maid of Orleans, they are being tortured and done to death, in the name of the King, in the name of the Church, and with the full knowledge and responsibility of established Government. At this very hour the leader of these fighters in the army of liberation is being held in prison and tortured."

As soon as the woman had begun to speak attendants had hurried around to the box. They found the door locked and barricaded from the inside, and by the time they had managed to break in she had finished her speech.

While the woman and two companions were being hurried out of the opera house there were cries of "Shame!" from among the audience. A great many people were less sympathetic, however. No one, they argued, was being tortured. If the suffragettes didn't struggle while they were being forcibly fed they would not be hurt. And, as for anyone being done to death, no one had died except poor Emily Wilding-Davison, and she had more or less killed herself. Some people thought that the suffragettes in prison should actually be allowed to starve to death. They were not pleased because the Home Secretary had said recently in the House of Commons that twenty women starving to death would become twenty martyrs, and that a great many people who now cared nothing about votes for women would then care very much indeed. Once roused, public opinion might oblige the Government to give way, and yielding to force was the last thing the Government intended to do.

Meanwhile, in the opera house, before the audience had time to settle back into their seats for the second act, forty women who had been quietly sitting in an upper gallery rose and showered suffragette pamphlets on to the heads of the people below. It was more than half an hour before this second disturbance was quelled and the opera was allowed to continue.

Early the next year—1914—Emmeline managed another trip to Paris. With her was Sylvia, who had crossed the Channel in disguise. Mother and daughter, who had been in prison so often, looked like ghosts, but both were prepared to go on defying the law to the end.

Christabel had asked them to come over to discuss fresh plans for the future. She herself now believed that the party most likely to give women the vote was the Conservative. But Sylvia, who had formed branches of the W.S.P.U. in the East End of London where she was dearly loved by working men and women, was a strong Socialist. It seemed to Christabel, who all this time had been guiding the militant campaign from Paris, that the time had come to part company. After a long discussion, it was agreed that she and her mother should continue to lead the W.S.P.U., while Sylvia's branches should become a separate body calling itself the East London Federation.

When this had been decided the family conference broke up, and this time Emmeline managed to evade the detectives waiting for her at Dover and get back to London before she was rearrested.

It was now becoming exceedingly difficult for suffragettes to hire any hall for a meeting. Emmeline would sometimes make speeches from convenient balconies at the houses of her friends. After one of these informal meetings she tried the veiled woman trick again and, as on the last occasion, it worked and the wrong woman was arrested. Emmeline herself was on her way to Glasgow when the trick was discovered. There, her followers had managed to hire a hall, and Emmeline, who had arrived quite safely, entered unobserved like any member of the audience. As soon as the police discovered she was there they rushed the hall. A free fight broke out in which the police at first got the worst of it. The suffragettes had hidden buckets of water and flowerpots behind the decorations on the platform and pelted the enemy until their ammunition was exhausted.

The police then made their arrests, and Emmeline was taken back to Holloway. She had protested so much about the coarse prison clothes that she was now allowed to wear her own. On this occasion she had on a favorite velvet dress which had been torn in the struggle. She refused to change it, and as a protest against the injustice of the whole situation, she lay down on the floor of her cell in it for three days. "It was dreadful to have it mauled and torn," she wrote afterward to Ethel Smyth, "and then to lie on the floor in it from Monday to Thursday. Such a becoming dress too!"

She was only in prison a few days this time, but before she left Holloway she had made up her mind to lead a delegation to the King at Buckingham Palace. They would petition him to use his influence to stop the ill treatment of suffragettes, and urge on him that the women of England had a right to vote. No group could be received by the King without the advice of the Home Office. The Home Office refused to advise him to receive them, but Emmeline resolved to go ahead all the same.

The group which set out for Buckingham Palace on May 21, 1914, was soon in difficulties. The police behaved very much as they had on Black Friday, hitting and punching the women for quite a long time before actually arresting them. In all the confusion Emmeline passed unnoticed almost to the Palace gates. There she was seized by an enormous police inspector, who picked her up bodily and gripped her so tightly that her ribs were bruised.

Of course she was sent back to prison, and with her went the others who had been arrested. It was a year now since she had been convicted, but out of that year she had served only thirty days of her three-year sentence. The remainder of the sentence stretched endlessly ahead if she continued to hunger- and thirst-strike—which, needless to say, she would do.

Prison was even harder to bear this time. From the adjoining cells Emmeline could hear the pitiful cries and struggles of her loyal followers as they were forcibly fed. Many of them were girls who had been militant for the first time, but not one of them had quailed. She remembered especially one young girl who had thrown herself repeatedly into the struggle, crying out as she did so, "Mrs. Pankhurst told us not to go back."

"My splendid ones!" Emmeline called her militants. She knew the moment they were released they would be militant again, and that when they went on hunger and thirst strikes they would again be forcibly fed. They gloried in their militant acts, but their leader could not altogether forgive herself for their sufferings. "It is all very well for me," she told Ethel Smyth afterward. "I have the limelight, but these . . ."

Outside prison all sorts of militant acts continued. One protest—against the sufferings of the prisoners—was actually made to the King in person. Wearing her court dress and ostrich feather headdress a debutante went with her mother and other debutantes to Buckingham Palace to be presented to the King and Queen. She swept a deep curtsy to the King and, as she rose, cried out, "For God's sake, Your Majesty, put a stop to this forcible feeding."

The girl was hurried away and, although the King made no sign that he had heard, everybody, including the girl's mother, was acutely embarrassed.

In the summer the National Union of Suffrage Societies organized a monster demonstration in Hyde Park. Through the years an ever-growing number of people—men as well as women—had come to the conclusion that women ought to have the vote. Government opposition at last began to crumble; and when Sylvia Pankhurst led a group of working women to the Prime Minister, she was not turned back or arrested. Instead, the women were received by Mr. Asquith, who seemed to accept the fact that sooner or later they must be given the vote.

The demonstrations of the suffrage societies had a tremendous effect on public opinions, but Emmeline had no hope that the end would be gained by peaceful methods alone. Nor did she trust the hints and half promises of members of the Government. "They must give us the vote," she cried passionately after her tenth hunger strike, "or they must give us death."

CHAPTER 13

A Double Victory

AT the beginning of August, 1914, Germany overran neutral Belgium, and Britain and France went to war with Germany in defense of Belgium.

On August 4, when war was declared, Emmeline was in France, having a short rest before her next bout of imprisonment. Christabel, who had spent the last two years in Paris, joined her mother at St. Malo, where she was staying so that between them they could decide on the right course for the W.S.P.U. to take.

"Winning the war must come first," said Emmeline. "Votes for women must wait till Germany is defeated. After all, what would be the good of a vote without a country to vote in?"

Christabel agreed. "We must call a truce for the duration of the war," she said, "and we can all do war work till the war is over."

On orders from their leaders the suffragettes stopped their militant acts. The Government responded by ordering the release of all the suffragettes still in prison. "His Majesty is confident," said the Home Secretary, "that they can be trusted not to stain the cause they have at heart by any further crime or disorder."

Sylvia Pankhurst disagreed with her mother and Christabel, and so did Adela. They were pacifists, who believed strongly that war was wrong. Adela had gone to live in Australia before the outbreak of war, but Sylvia, although she disapproved of war, spent the war years at home trying to reduce its bad effects, helping to open infant welfare centers and day nurseries in the East End of London.

The need for men to join the fighting forces meant that there was soon an acute shortage of munition workers at home. As everybody knew, the war could not be won without ammunition.

Emmeline Pankhurst was surprised one day to get a message from Lloyd George, who was now Minister of Munitions, asking her to come and see him. She went and for the first time met her old enemy on equal terms.

The Minister outlined the position to her. "Briefly, the position is this," he said. "We shan't be able to solve the munitions shortage unless we can get women into the factories to take the place of the men who are being called up."

"That shouldn't be very difficult."

"I'm not so sure, Mrs. Pankhurst. There is a good deal of opposition to the idea of women working in munitions factories."

"You don't think I'm opposed to it myself?"

Lloyd George smiled. "Of course not. But I want to suggest to you that you should organize a procession of women, like the processions you used to have for the vote.

This one won't be for the vote; it will show that women are willing and ready for the work."

"But everyone knows that women are ready," objected Emmeline.

"Yes, I know. But I want the right atmosphere created to convince our opponents that this is the only way. The procession should end in a delegation to me, as Minister of Munitions, asking me to open the factories to women."

It was an odd situation for Emmeline to be invited by the Government to organize a procession, and she smiled a little grimly to herself. However, she would not refuse. "Very well," she said, "I will see what I can do."

It was not difficult to arrange a procession with the help of unlimited money to pay for the hiring of bands and the printing of banners and handbills. And a number of newspapers carried articles praising the women for their patriotism instead of snarling at them as lawbreakers, as they had done in the old days.

Emmeline herself led the group, which was received by Mr. Winston Churchill, then First Lord of the Admiralty, as well as by Mr. Lloyd George. When Emmeline told them that the women of England demanded to be allowed to work in munitions factories, both Ministers gladly agreed to do their best to make this possible.

The opposition then died away and for the remainder of the war women did splendid work, not only in munitions factories but in all the other forms of war work which were opened to them. The capable way in which they took over jobs to release men for the forces made many employers ashamed that women were still denied the right to vote. Things were at long last moving in the right direction. Emmeline herself could not believe that when the war was over the Government would continue to refuse women political freedom.

She was exceedingly busy at the time addressing recruiting meetings all over the country. But in addition to her public work she decided to do something for children orphaned by the war. She therefore rented a house in Holland Park in London and furnished it with the help of the faithful Nurse Pine, who had nursed her back to health so often in the past. She adored small children and was thrilled at the prospect of setting up house again.

"All these years I have persuaded myself that I did not want a home of my own," she wrote to Ethel Smyth, who was working in a hospital in France. "But now that I can have one I am all impatience to get into it."

Four baby girls were brought into the household. Everything went well at first, but Emmeline, who had never had any money sense, did not realize what an expense the children would be. She had hoped that her friends would help her, but few of them did, for they disapproved of her scheme. She had never kept money for herself, so now, although she was getting old, she decided to go on another lecture tour of America. Most of the money she made was to go toward the war effort. She was to keep the proceeds from certain lectures for herself.

In the end, she impulsively gave more money than she had promised to the war effort, and the difficulties of running the household continued.

She had not been back from America very long when

the Government at last showed signs of giving women the vote. In the spring of 1917, when the country was still in the thick of war, Lloyd George, who was now Prime Minister, asked members of the various suffrage organizations to meet him at 10 Downing Street. The Government, he told them, was ready to introduce a reform bill which would give some, if not all, women the vote.

"Whatever you think can be passed," Emmeline told him, "we are ready to accept."

The reform bill which got through Parliament gave the vote to women of thirty and over. This was a great victory for the patient, law-abiding suffragists as well as for the militant suffragettes.

There was very little opposition to the bill in the House of Commons, but it had yet to be debated in the House of Lords when Emmeline, who no longer had any fear of the future, went on a visit to Russia. Revolution had broken out in March, 1917, in which the Czar, the ruler of the whole of Russia, had been overthrown. And then, after a short period of intense confusion, a Soviet Government took over and Communism became Russia's official way of life.

Emmeline was extremely interested in the rise of the Russian workers, and was very glad of the chance to see something of the situation for herself. She went as a sort of unofficial messenger from the British Government, and arrived during the period of confusion.

Russia, who had come into the war on the side of the Allies, had now withdrawn and signed a peace treaty with Germany. The British Government was anxious to bring

Russia back into the war, and so Emmeline and a number of other influential people went there to see if they could do anything about it. They failed, but from all they saw, they were convinced that it would not be long before Soviet rule was established.

Emmeline was back in London just before the end of the year. On January 18, 1918, the reform bill became law. The day she had waited for so long had arrived at last.

On February 6 a great meeting was held in Albert Hall, the scene of many stormy meetings in past years. Emmeline appeared on the platform with Christabel and other suffragette leaders. Although the enthusiasm was great, the meeting was a quiet one. For years Emmeline had dreamed of the triumphant rejoicings which would follow victory; but the other victory—over Germany—had still to be won, and no one had the heart to triumph while so many people were being killed.

Looking into the future, she spoke of the peacetime fight which would follow the war, the fight to gain equal opportunity for men and women. "We must be given the same chance as men to qualify in all the professions," she said. "To continue to work in the factories, but not for such long hours that we cannot enjoy the leisure which peace will bring." She spoke, too, of the need to bring mechanical aids into the home so that women could be freed from drudgery. But although her ideas seem obvious today, they were new then and her audience was still too war-weary to show real interest. For the first time Emmeline's voice seemed to have lost its magic, and her audience did not thrill to her words. It was true that she was growing old and very tired, but it was also true that she herself was only really fired by the "Votes for Women" cause.

Women were gaining their parliamentary rights swiftly now. In November, 1918, Germany was defeated and the four years' war was brought to an end. Within a few weeks of victory a bill had been rushed through Parliament which enabled women to stand as candidates for election to the House of Commons.

A general election had been fixed for mid-December, which gave the women very little time to prepare. All the same, there were seventeen women candidates in the field. Only one—Countess Markievicz—was successful. She was elected as a Sinn Feiner. The Sinn Fein was the organization which supported the Republican Party of Ireland, the whole of which was still part of the British Isles, and like the seventy-two other Sinn Feiners elected, she never took her seat.

The list of unsuccessful women candidates was headed by Christabel Pankhurst. Emmeline had worked tirelessly for her daughter, and it was a great disappointment to her that Christabel did not become the first woman member of Parliament.

CHAPTER 14

A Niche in the Temple of Fame

Now that women's right to vote had been won Emmeline's real work was done. Her influence over her followers had been very powerful. They had supported her most loyally, and had committed militant acts and hunger-struck in prison without thought of the consequences. She was certainly something of a tyrant, as most leaders are, but she had called for no sacrifice from her followers that she was not willing to make herself.

For many suffragettes life must have seemed a little flat when the fight was over. To Emmeline, who was sixty by the end of the war, the need was to find work to provide for the four children in her home. Canada and the United States offered the best chance of earning a living, she thought, and she sailed from England in the autumn of 1919, leaving the little girls in Nurse Pine's care. In Canada she was given an official job as lecturer on public-health questions, a job which took her all over the country. As soon as she could afford it she sent for Nurse Pine and the children. The family party was joined by Christabel, who had given up politics after her defeat as a parliamentary candidate.

Emmeline loved Canada and meant to settle there. Nurse Pine was desperately homesick for England, but she refused to desert Mrs. Pankhurst. When the children were old enough to start lessons Emmeline engaged a governess for them, and Nurse Pine stayed on to do the housework and cooking.

The job lasted several years, but as Emmeline grew older, she found the constant traveling and lecturing more and more tiring. Finally her health broke down and she had to apply for leave of absence. The whole household moved to Bermuda, and Emmeline, who soon began to get well in the peace and sunshine, spent much time teaching the children to swim.

But by this time she was sixty-seven and she knew that the task of supporting the children until they grew up was beyond her. Good homes in England were found for two of them, Christabel adopted the third, and Emmeline was left with Mary, her favorite among the little girls.

She could not remain idle in Bermuda forever, and she did not feel that she could endure the cold of the Canadian winters any longer. With Mary and Nurse Pine, she went back to England.

For a time she stayed in London with a much younger sister, Mrs. Goulden-Bach. Sylvia, meeting her mother again after six years, found her looking withered and frail, though still beautiful.

Although she was old and tired the offer of a job in politics brought Emmeline back to life. She had in the past belonged to the Liberal and the Labor parties, but in her old age she was a staunch Conservative. When she was invited to stand for Parliament as a Conservative candidate she eagerly accepted. The seat she was to fight at the next general election—Whitechapel and St. George's in the East End of London—was a safe Labor seat, but the Conservative authorities thought that if anybody could bring down the Labor vote it would be Emmeline Pankhurst.

When she started working in her constituency all her energy seemed to come back. People who heard her speak for the first time were conquered by the magic of her personality and her voice.

A Conservative Government was in power at the time under Stanley Baldwin, and the Government was bringing in a bill that would extend the vote to all women twenty-one and over. When this bill became law, and there was no doubt that it would, men and women would at last be free to vote on absolutely equal terms. The Prime Minister was to speak on the measure at a meeting in Albert Hall, and to Emmeline's delight, she was asked to move a vote of thanks to him. Although she spoke without the aid of a microphone, her voice was as clear as ever and her words could be heard in the highest gallery.

Emmeline threw herself into her election campaign with typical impulsiveness. She addressed meetings, called on her constituents, opened bazaars, and did all the other jobs which parliamentary candidates are called on to do. But by now she was often so ill and weary that she could scarcely drag herself from one meeting to the next. Yet the moment she mounted the platform her old fire returned, and after her long experience as a heckler she was able to make short work of anyone who attempted to heckle her.

As she thought it would be less tiring and give her a better chance of success to live in her constituency, she left her sister's home for rooms in the East End. The rooms were mean and cramped and reminded her a little of a prison cell. "I hate small rooms," she cried, flinging wide her arms, but she knew she would have to get used to them.

The move meant parting from Mary, the last of the children. But Mary now needed to go to school and to have more care than Emmeline could give her. A home was therefore found for the child, and Emmeline was on her own. She missed Mary desperately, and she loathed the poverty and squalor of the East End. Yet all through her life, once she had made up her mind to do something she never turned back, and she was not going to change now.

She had spent only a short time in her rooms when she was taken ill.

"It's not serious, I hope," said a friend who came to see her and found her in bed in the tiny bedroom.

"It's nothing," said Emmeline. "I've been ill on and off for years, and all those weeks of hunger striking didn't improve my digestion."

"Is there anything I can do?"

Emmeline shook her head. "My landlady is looking after me perfectly. She's one of the kindest women I've ever met, and although I thought at first I should never get used to these small rooms I know now I shall be happy here."

"What does the doctor say?" asked her friend.

"I've seen two doctors and neither of them thinks it's anything serious. There's really nothing at all the matter with me that a few days' rest won't cure."

Yet as the days went by Emmeline grew worse instead of better. "If only I could get my strength back," she told her friend. "I know I've got five years of good work in me yet."

But though she rallied for a short while, Emmeline's working days were over. So too was the long struggle to which she had given so many years of her life, for in 1928, during this last illness, the final stages of the bill which gave the vote to women of twenty-one were passed. On July 2 the act received the Royal Assent and became law. But by that time Emmeline Pankhurst was dead.

She had died on June 14, a month before her seventieth birthday. The night before the funeral a little band of her faithful, militant suffragettes kept watch over the coffin which rested in St. John's Church, Smith Square, Westminster. Next morning there was a service in the church, and then a long procession of Emmeline's old comrades followed the coffin to Brompton cemetery. The crowd which had gathered in Smith Square was silent, and as the coffin was carried out of the church the police stood at attention and saluted.

Just under two years after Emmeline's death, on March 6, 1930, a statue of her was unveiled by Prime Minister Stanley Baldwin. The statue stood in the Victoria Tower

Gardens, Westminster, close to the Houses of Parliament, the scene of so many of her struggles.

Her admirers gathered in full force to pay their leader this last tribute. Beside the veiled statue two platforms had been set up and hung with the purple, white, and green of the suffragette colors. One platform was for the speakers—Stanley Baldwin, "General" Flora Drummond, Mr. Pethick-Lawrence, and Lady Rhondda, a former militant and founder of the weekly paper *Time and Tide*. The other platform was for the band of the Metropolitan Police, who gladly joined in the tribute to their former enemy. On the platform with the speakers were politicians, some of whom had also been Emmeline's enemies in the past, and among the crowd of women who pressed about the platforms the suffragette colors were everywhere to be seen, in ribbons, wreaths, and bouquets.

Before the ceremony began the police band, conducted by its director of music, played music which included several compositions by women. As the speakers climbed onto the platform the director gave up his place to a woman, and Ethel Smyth stepped up to conduct her "March of the Women."

When Stanley Baldwin, square-jawed and kindly faced, got to his feet he stood looking about him for several moments before he began to speak. There was something very English, he said at last, in a ceremony which was taking place in the presence of men and women of all political parties to honor a woman who had spent much of her life in bitter political strife. "We are united today," he went on, "to dedicate this monument in the very shadow of our Houses of Parliament, and it has fallen to my lot—one who for many years was opposed to the work that Mrs. Pankhurst was doing—to put the coping-stone upon her labors."

It was still too early to see the militant campaign and its leaders in their true perspective. "But I say with no fear of contradiction, that whatever view posterity may take, Mrs. Pankhurst has won for herself a niche in the temple of fame which will last for all time."

Mr. Baldwin went on to speak of the long struggle in which so many women—nonmilitant as well as militant—had played a part. Among them, he said, Mrs. Pankhurst stood out as "a leader of power and of magnetism, a woman who was a natural orator, a prophet, and . . . a despot."

Women now had their political rights, and it was for them to show that they could use them well. In the years to come, "no woman as she passes this place will fail to draw inspiration from the example and the courage of the heroic woman whose statue we today unveil and whose memory we are here to honor."

Emmeline's statue was unveiled to a fanfare of trumpets, and the base was heaped high with flowers.

Today, while some women take their political rights for granted, there are many others who do not forget how bitterly those rights were won. Emmeline Pankhurst's statue is still a place of pilgrimage; in 1958, the centenary year of her birth, an addition was decided on in memory of Christabel, who had died during the year. The addition takes the form of two low walls, each ending in a pier with a bronze medallion. One medallion shows a bronze relief of Christabel—the other the brooch worn by members of the W.S.P.U. who had suffered imprisonment. The opening ceremony was performed by Lord Kilmuir, the Lord Chancellor, on July 13, 1959, and it is indeed fitting that mother and daughter should be commemorated by the same monument.

More recently still—in 1960—two more suffragette memorials were unveiled. The first was a plaque in the Free Trade Hall, Manchester, which commemorates the meeting of October 13, 1905, when Christabel Pankhurst and Annie Kenney became the first suffragettes to go to prison and the long militant struggle began. The second was a plaque, unveiled by the famous actress Dame Sybil Thorndike, on the wall of the old suffragette headquarters in Clement's Inn.

We may not all of us approve of Emmeline's violent methods; we may even believe that the vote would have been won just as soon by the suffragists who worked without violence. But we cannot deny that Emmeline was an immensely brave and single-minded woman, who inspired her followers with a courage equal to her own.

Bibliography

Adams, Mildred, *The Right to Be People,* Philadelphia, J. B. Lippincott Co., 1966.

Coolidge, Olivia, *Women's Rights,* New York, E. P. Dutton & Co., 1966.

Faber, Doris, *Petticoat Politics: How American Women Won the Right to Vote,* New York, Lothrop, Lee & Shepard Co., 1967.

Flexner, Eleanor, *Century of Struggle: The Woman's Rights Movement in the United States,* Cambridge, Mass., Harvard University Press, 1959.

Foster, G. Allen, *Votes for Women,* New York, Criterion Books, Inc., 1966.

Grimes, Alan P., *The Puritan Ethic and Woman Suffrage,* New York, Oxford University Press, 1967.

Katzenstein, Caroline, *Lifting the Curtain,* Philadelphia, Dorrance & Co., 1955.

Kraditor, Aileen W., *The Ideas of the Woman Suffrage Movement, 1890–1920,* New York, Columbia University Press, 1965.

Mitchell, David, *The Fighting Pankhursts: A Study in Tenacity,* New York, The Macmillan Company, 1967.

Severn, Bill, *Free But Not Equal: How Women Won the Right to Vote,* New York, Julian Messner, 1967.